KATE GARRAWAY

was born 50ish years ago in Abingdon-on-Thames, Oxfordshire. A busy wife and mum-of-two, she can usually be found throughout the week on the sofa of ITV's *Good Morning Britain* or hosting her own daily radio show on Global's *Smooth Radio*.

Having worked in television on the BBC, Sky and ITV for nearly 20 years, she has interviewed all of the biggest names in the world of entertainment, including Tom Cruise, Johnny Depp and Meryl Streep. Along with every Prime Minister since Margaret Thatcher. You can follow her on Twitter @kategarraway.

PRAISE FOR
The Joy of BIG KNICKERS

'*The Joy of Big Knickers* is full of advice for blooming into midl

'Warm, funny and refr
Garraway's literary debut of
of aging... Packed with expert advice' *OK!* magazine

'Upbeat, positive and humorous' *Belfast Telegraph*

'Moving and hilarious' *Best* magazine

'Kate Garraway is smart, down-to-earth and great fun. In her first book ... [she] brings her no-nonsense charm to the business of aging gracefully' *Bristol Post*

'[Kate's] embraced her most cringe-worthy moments and written a book about the lessons she's learnt approaching middle age' *Daily Mail*

'A delightfully candid delve into [Kate's] "midlife moments", where she shares everything from embracing "sausage-skin" undies to facelift fears and marital heartbreak' *LoveSunday* magazine

The Joy of BIG KNICKERS

(OR LEARNING TO LOVE THE REST OF YOUR LIFE)

KATE GARRAWAY

Published by Blink Publishing
3.08, The Plaza,
535 Kings Road,
Chelsea Harbour,
London, SW10 0SZ

www.blinkpublishing.co.uk

facebook.com/blinkpublishing
twitter.com/blinkpublishing

Hardback – 978-1-911-274-48-3
Trade paperback – 978-1-911-274-49-0
Paperback – 978-1-911-274-47-6
Ebook – 978-1-911-274-50-6

A CIP catalogue of this book is available from the British Library.

Design and typeset by seagulls.net
Printed and bound by Clays Ltd, St. Ives Plc

1 3 5 7 9 10 8 6 4 2

First published in 2017 by Blink Publishing
First published in paperback in 2017 by Blink Publishing

Blink Publishing is an imprint of the Bonnier Publishing Group
www.bonnierpublishing.co.uk

For my amazing family and friends
– thank you – you are the best of my world.

ACKNOWLEDGEMENTS

Thank you to my wonderfully supportive husband for putting up with me banging on about this book for the last few months, and for living and loving my midlife moments with me – you are the love of my life. Thank you to Darcy and Billy for letting me dominate the computer when you wanted to be on YouTube and for the extraordinary joy you bring every day. I am so proud of you. Thank you to my mum, dad and brother, Matthew, for everything over the last 49 years, and to the rest of my family for being a constant source of inspiration and comfort. Thank you to Chrina and Ken and all the Drapers for their constant love and support.

To my friends who tolerated me calling them at all hours of the day and night, and to everyone at Roar Global, particularly Grant, Rebecca, Kate and Jonathan – you made this book happen. Thank you to the clever Dundas Communications team; Max, Cal and Amy, for helping me spread 'The Joy of Big Knickers'. To the fabulous Helen Warner and Rebecca Cripps – you are the best sounding boards ever, even though I may have driven you doolally in the process – thanks for helping me find the right words when I struggled. Thanks to all the gang at *GMB*. To my editor, Neil Thompson, for your amazing support and advice, and Emma Gormley, for two decades of fun and guidance. Ben for your wit and wisdom, Susanna for your nurturing support. Charlotte for helping me research stuff when you should have been focusing on reading the news (shh, no one will ever know!). And to Ranvir, Richard, Piers, Laura and Sean and all the rest on and off screen for being a total joy and blessing every day.

Thanks to the team at Smooth Radio and, particularly, to the brilliant and saintly Dave Brierley-Jones, who has to put up with me for three hours everyday – I can't imagine how annoying it was hearing all about my midlife at 25! Thank you Martin Lewis for your advice and friendship, and Annie Penny for your life-changing talents. Huge thanks to the legions who hit midlife before me and whose written testimonies and insights have helped me to make my way through my own maelstrom. And huge thanks to the whole Blink Publishing team – a nicer, cleverer bunch of people you couldn't hope to meet.

Contents

CHAPTER 1

Hello and Welcome!

'Hello and welcome to *The Joy of Big Knickers*!'

Once a TV presenter, always a TV presenter.

You may doubt me now, but I am hoping that by the end of this book you will also share my joy in big knickers (occasionally seen in full view on breakfast TV and pretty much worn every day). What can I say? They're one of my staples! And, like many other things I reveal in this book, are one of my secrets to feeling great about myself every day. They are just for me, and not to prove myself to anyone else. But now I want to share all my secrets with you! As I turned fifty I tried to make sense of what I now truly believe is an astonishing and wonderful era of life.

I would love you to join me as I embrace midlife madness and discover the genuine magic I have found it holds: fighting and beating the scourge of sagging skin (well, sagging everything really!), skipping along the trail of real romance, and locating those hidden gems embedded within the ups and downs of later life.

Did I mention death? Well, that also.

So, yes, I'm hoping you will keep me company as we learn to love the rest of our lives in a wonderful and magical way – as I know we can. TRUST ME.

I know what you're thinking – of course that Kate Garraway can learn to love the rest of HER life. What's not to love? She's got an amazing job that has taken her to exciting and exclusive places all over the world, rubbing shoulder pads with the most glamorous of A-listers. She has a strong marriage, two gorgeous kids, seems in good health – and if ever she is having a fat day, a bad hair day or a 'what's that looking back at me in the mirror?' day, her job in television means that there is always a team of experts on hand to bring out her slick and shiny self.

Well, I can't deny it – behind the smoke and mirrors are some really talented folk keeping up my TV appearance, even if it's taking a lot longer nowadays. Keep reading because these fabulous trade secrets will be yours to help you shine!

These days, though, I am realising that despite the daily transformation in the make-up room, the passage of time is lurching forward faster than I can even speak (and let's be honest, that's really fast – the word chatterbox was invented for me!).

It's also true that everyone, however fortunate, has a moment when they realise that this so-called passage of time is changing them, and perhaps not in a good way.

This moment of realisation for me began as a heart-thumping thought that developed into a stream of consciousness that became a conversation – because, as I say, I'm an eternal chatterbox – and it was a conversation I began to share with numerous people: some of whom were experts, who gave me brilliant advice; some, inspirational famous faces, who I have met along the way in twenty-five years of TV; and others, friends, who were dealing with their own midlife moments, in their own way.

By the way, I am resisting the urge to call it a midlife crisis, because that conjures up all sorts of clichés of men with overly trendy hairdos, driving cars they can't afford and dating women young enough to be their daughters. Or women sporting too-short skirts, taking up pole dancing and having wild affairs with younger men. Not that the latter isn't appealing! But I have found that midlife moments come in all manner of strange and confusing forms.

You might, for instance, find yourself almost catatonic with exhaustion – running around like mad, working too hard trying to make ends meet, looking after your family, caring for older relatives and barely noticing your partner, other than to remind each other of the jobs you have failed to do as you fall into bed at the end of the day, too tired even to wonder where the fun in your life has gone.

Or you might be thinking, OK, things are going pretty well so far, but how do I keep it up? Is this the best it's going to get? And if I can't sustain it, what will happen to me as I get older?

You might be wondering how you and your partner will fare as your looks change and health worries creep in. Or you might find yourself lying alone in bed asking, 'How did love pass me by?' or 'Why did they leave again?'

Maybe you feel as if you're living in the classic Talking Heads song of the 1980s, 'Once in a Lifetime', waking up and puzzling over why your life hasn't worked out how you planned. You, too, may find yourself asking where that large automobile and beautiful house you thought you'd have by now has got to. And wondering, as they do in the song, if you have been just letting the days of your life go by.

Whatever our 'midlife moments', I have learnt that this is not a time to just 'let the days go by' and bury our heads in the sand. Far from the stagnant, boring, dull image that middle agers often get tagged with, I think midlife is a time of

EXPLOSIVE CHANGE.

Let us not allow ourselves to sleepwalk into the next chunk of life – one minute being fifty, the next seventy. It would be criminal to miss out on so many potential new experiences and the wonderful feelings that are part of that package.

Midlife, I believe, is a critical period. A time to take charge and excel at the things we never knew we could be any good at; to accept what is gone and shore ourselves up for the future. Let's not drift regretfully into old age, full of bitterness about the things we didn't do, wishing we'd taken more risks, or fewer risks. Wishing we had done things differently.

A century ago, middle age was often the end of life. Now it is the start of a new phase that can extend to thirty years or more. Historically, these are unchartered waters. Society can't dictate what we should do, because we are among the first to do it.

How utterly liberating!

Just as in puberty when our hormones rage and we start taking risks, experimenting and throwing off the confines of childhood, so too in midlife we have to throw off the first half of our lives. The old rules don't work any more. The people who used to tell us what to do – people like our parents, teachers and bosses – can no longer show us the way, even if we want them to.

Our parents are likely to need more and more of our care, if we are lucky enough still to have them. Our teachers are no longer around and our bosses, frankly, are getting younger and younger – and so less likely to relate to where we are at.

Added to that, if you are a woman, the parallel with puberty is even stronger. Hormonal changes surge through our bodies and minds as the menopause begins to make its presence known. Sometimes we get lost in the bonkers, going from rational to rash and ending up in the radical – whether that's a marriage breakdown or a career change (not all bad, I hear you say). Yes, I am all for an impulsive ticket to a foreign clime, a trek up Kilimanjaro or braving a bungee jump down a ravine, but does responding to these urges actually answer our big questions? Or begin to solve our problems?

Creating a bucket list of crazy stuff is great, but perhaps only fulfiling if interspersed with other more important and intimate things. A romantic evening with a partner, old or new? Unlocking the code to a meaningful conversation with our teenage child? Awakening the sex gods and goddesses within? Finding the funds to fulfill our wildest dreams? Discovering what our true dreams actually are? Rediscovering ways to enjoy our own company and those who we used to really like?

This book is about working out my life list, rather than a bucket list. It's a recipe for cooking up the ingredients for the best rest of my life. You may find something that resonates with your own life – I don't think any of us are so very different, even if it can look that way from the outside. Or you may choose to forge your own path through this unchartered territory, and that's fine too. But either way I hope you enjoy my comical, calamitous and sometimes scary attempts to face the challenges of midlife head on.

As it has been said on the big reality shows numerous times, it's been quite a 'journey' so far – and, after all, what bigger and better reality show is there than the rest of our lives?

It all started for me with a very big wake-up call ...

CHAPTER 2

The Wake-up Call

MONDAY MORNING, 8 AUGUST 2016

'It's probably nothing,' I told my GP on the phone, in the time-honoured way that all British people start a conversation with their doctor.

We were moving house and I'd been packing up boxes and lugging them up and down stairs all week. They say that after the really grim duo, bereavement and divorce, moving is the most stressful thing you can do – and I was seriously feeling the effects. By the weekend I'd started to feel crushing pains in my chest whenever I took a breath.

What's going on? I thought. Is it some kind of anxiety attack, indigestion (hoping) or – *gulp* – is it my heart? My lungs?

By Monday morning there was no ignoring the pains – sharp stabbing ones now, making it agony to breathe in or out. My chest was feeling tighter by the minute and I was out of breath just climbing the stairs. Oh my God, I thought, this is really bad.

I tried not to, but suddenly all I could think of was all the partying I'd done, all the nights I had stayed out until the early hours, drinking ill-advised but hugely fun sambuca shots, all the sleep I had missed by getting up at 2.15 a.m. for *Good Morning Britain* and other breakfast shows for the best part of two decades, and the fact that I hadn't exercised regularly for years. Maybe this was it – payback time. All my chickens coming home to roost.

I put in a call to my GP, where an efficient but weary-sounding receptionist put me into a callback system. 'I'm not sure that will work,' I said, 'because when the doctor calls back, I will be on-air doing my radio show on Smooth, so it will be hard for her to get through to me.'

'Do you want medical advice or not?' she asked tersely.

I did. I really did.

Sure enough, when the doctor called me back I was on air presenting my daily radio show. Despite how I was feeling, I fully expected her to be relaxed about my symptoms. I thought she might say, 'Maybe you should come in and see me later,' or 'See how you are in a couple of days and call me back.'

Instead, after asking me about my symptoms, she said, 'I'm looking at your age and charts: PUT THE PHONE DOWN NOW AND GO TO A&E.'

'Oh!' I said, breaking out in a cold sweat. 'But I'm on-air!'

'How important is your health to you?' she asked.

My heart began to race. 'I can't just walk out of the studio. It's just me here—'

'I think you should go straight to A&E,' she interrupted. 'That is my honest advice.'

It's not as though I wasn't already horribly aware of my age. I work in an industry where most people are way below fifty. I am older than most of my on-screen colleagues – and the ones behind the scenes, too – and ever since my fortieth birthday, people like my mate and Entertainment Editor at *Good Morning Britain*, Richard Arnold, have been teasing me about hurtling towards fifty and drowning in 'middle youth', all the while dropping hints about a creeping desperation and a tragic hanging on to what he calls 'extended adolescence'.

Then there was my forty-ninth birthday, only a few weeks before, when I'd headed to my radio show not expecting any kind of fuss – just happy that my age still began with a four – and walked into a bevvy of balloons, a cheer and a huge cake. How sweet, I thought – until I looked down at the cake and saw that it was emblazoned with 'HAPPY 50th KATE!' in bright pink.

As the non-fifty-year-olds say, hashtag awks.

'But I'm only forty-nine,' I said.

'No, you're not,' my producer, Dave Brierley-Jones, insisted – laughing but deadly serious.

'Er, yes, I am.'

He looked bemused. 'Really?' There was a pause. 'How annoying! To celebrate, I've spent ages putting together a playlist of songs with references to the number fifty. Like "Fifty Ways to Leave Your Lover".'

He was annoyed? Being young, like the rest of the Smooth team, at twenty-four he didn't realise that adding a year to a woman's age is almost as bad as offering her a seat because you think she's expecting, only to find out it's pasta not pregnancy. At forty-nine, you want people to think you are at least a decade younger, not a year older!

But this was different. These sharp pains weren't so much about hurt pride. This felt like an age-related medical crisis.

Nevertheless I finished the radio show – no point giving in to full panic – and made my way to the nearest hospital. By the time I got there, the pain seemed to have crept up from my chest to my neck and was seriously constricting my throat. I was white and clammy. The staff took one look at me, heard my symptoms and then efficiently whizzed me in for tests on my heart and lungs. (Would they have done that if I were twenty with the same symptoms, I wondered?) Thankfully an ECG quickly established that I wasn't having a heart attack.

Relief. While I was waiting for my chest X-ray results, a consultant came over to examine me. The second he pressed my chest, I jumped, yelped and nearly shot off the table.

'Ah,' he said. 'You're going to be fine. This is muscular – you've torn the cartilage around your ribs. Have you overdone it at the gym?'

I laughed, possibly for the first time that day. 'Does going five years ago count as overdoing it? I've been twice in a decade, which is probably too much for me.'

He smiled thinly. 'Not the gym, then.'

'But I have just moved house,' I said. 'I've been carting boxes around all weekend.'

'That will be it,' he said. 'You have to be careful as you get older.'

Oh, those roosting chickens.

He didn't stop there. 'You have to realise that you're not twenty-five,' he chided. 'You're not even thirty-five.'

I felt like clapping my hands over my ears.

'You're forty-nine and you are at that age where if you don't look after your body it won't look after you,' he added.

Thanks, Dr Opposite-of-Feelgood! Never mind suspected cardiac arrest, or even torn cartilage around the ribcage: that was a stab to the heart.

But of course it wasn't so much his words that hurt as the shocking fact that my body in its current state couldn't cope with lifting a few boxes, and his lack of surprise at this fact. I obviously felt huge relief that there wasn't something seriously wrong with my heart and lungs, but there was something about his manner that suggested I had got away with it this time. What was he really saying? That I should just accept creeping decrepitude? Seriously depressing! And what was the alternative?

Was I going to have to give up everything I loved and become one of those joy-sapping, boring, knit-your-own-yoghurt-and-eat-it gym bunnies, so desperate to stay looking and feeling young that they have no time or room left for any personality?

Now my heart really sank.

What to do? Well, what have I always done in any crisis, big or small?

Call in the 'girls'.

Now, don't get me wrong – the girls aren't all female. They are the mates I have collected over the years who know me really well; the mates I may not see for years, but when I do it feels like we're continuing a conversation we left off only yesterday. The mates I call on, whatever the situation, because they each have their own unique perspective.

Of course, they all had their views on what my 'trouble' was.

'Oh, your trouble is you have always been paranoid coming up to a big birthday,' said my old college mate, Joe. 'Don't you remember when we went for that picnic for your twentieth at college and you were moping about leaving your teens?'

Funny, I remember that as a really fun day, but I know what he meant. It's very easy to look back and think everything was better when you were younger. So, yes, at twenty, my body could take all sorts of punishment and my skin was as springy as a brand-new trampoline. But I was also fretting about spots, worrying about essays and whether I would ever get my degree, meet a boy who would want to marry me, get a job or have a life ...

By thirty, I had achieved quite a few of the things I'd hankered after: I'd made my way into journalism, got a brilliant new job hosting *Sunrise* on Sky News, found a man who, miracle of miracles, wanted to marry me and moved into a new home. Only trouble was, it all very quickly fell apart. I was left heartbroken and spent the best part of the next decade crying, trying to work out what had gone wrong and my part in it, constantly fighting a fear that at some deep level I was unloveable.

Then, slowly, with the help of friends and family, a lot of late nights and wine, I pieced myself back together, tried dating again – finding it fun now that I was clearer about what I wanted – and by thirty-seven

I had met my wonderful, colourful, drives-me-crazy-but-I-adore-him new husband, Derek, and within a year we were married and expecting our first baby. So when forty came around, I felt nothing but happiness and relief that I had salvaged my life while still fertile enough to have the family I had always dreamt of.

There also seemed to be loads of new things to look forward to: watching my little two-year-old daughter Darcey grow, helping her develop and hopefully going on to have a second child. There were new career opportunities – by now I was working at *GMTV* and loving it. Then came BBC's *Strictly Come Dancing* – sparkle, glamour and primetime fame (despite my clear hopelessness at the actual dancing). Following that, I had the chance to make a documentary for Channel 4 on breastfeeding, which took me to America to meet new, fascinating people, like the man who believed breast milk had cured his cancer. I was convinced the producers wouldn't have asked me to lead that show had I not just become a mum and recently had experience of breastfeeding. Back then it felt the passage of time and the phases of life I was moving through – like motherhood – were all creating new opportunities, widening my horizons and bringing only positive change.

But fifty did not feel like a new beginning. In fact, it felt like the beginning of the end. For a start, there seemed to be less to look forward to. It felt as if all of society's boxes had been ticked. Think about it: when you're a kid, it's all about learning new things, making new friends, passing your exams, going to college, getting a job, finding a partner, settling down and having a family ... Once that's done, what's left? Trying to stay married, trying to keep your job and your finances going, waiting to become a grandparent? In my case, having had kids so late, if mine waited as long as I did I would be eighty before I even got a sniff of a grandchild.

What if I didn't even (*gulp*) make it that far?

Of course, I still had my wonderful job. I am very grateful to have a job that is exciting, demanding, endlessly fascinating and full of opportunities to meet new people with interesting stories to tell, famous or not. And I know just how lucky I am to have it. But for how long? TV and radio have always been competitive industries, but suddenly it felt like I was fighting off a new line of attack: youth. A surge of younger people coming up with more energy, new ideas and fewer personal and family responsibilities.

'It's all so exhausting,' I wailed. 'It's as if your birthdays are ganging up on you and rattling and ruining every area of your life.'

'Your trouble is you work in a world that isn't real,' said my friend Abi Donald. I have known Abi since I was twenty-two and walked into the then brand-new independent local radio station for Oxford, Fox FM. I was hoping they would let me do some unpaid work experience and Abi was kind enough to take me out with her on a story and show me the basics of radio editing and news broadcasting. We ended up working together on and off for the next twenty-seven years in various newsrooms around the country. She has now left the industry, so has an interesting perspective as she has worked both inside and outside it, and of course knows me really well.

'You interview a lot of Hollywood A-listers and glamorous TV stars, who spend all day working out and beautifying themselves, with the best help money can buy. These people don't look or behave like they're supposed to at fifty. It's not normal and you shouldn't be comparing yourself to them.'

'How are we fifty-year-olds SUPPOSED to look and behave, then?' I asked.

But I knew what she meant.

One of the perks of my job is meeting all sorts of incredible people and I have been lucky enough to interview some amazing women in their fifties. People like Halle Berry, who at forty-seven got pregnant with her son, Maceo, naturally – and when I met her had the skin of a twenty-year-old. And Sandra Bullock, who at fifty-three could easily pass for twenty years younger and has a body so toned and lithe it would shame an Olympian in their prime. Closer to home, among my

ITV colleagues, there's Lorraine Kelly at fifty-seven who, thanks to a new health regime and some great genes (I have met her mum), looks better than ever. Then there's my great mate Susanna Reid, a brilliant journalist with one of the fastest forensic brains you will ever come across – yet at forty-six she also has the raw sex appeal of a young Marilyn Monroe. She always jokes that she's been 'on the slide since forty-five'. Rubbish! When she hits the red carpet, she blows everyone away. And what about the gorgeous Charlotte Hawkins? I swear she must have a picture stored somewhere in an attic. I mean, how is it even possible to have skin that flawless at forty-one?

Don't even get me started on Davina McCall who, as she was approaching fifty, ran, swam and cycled from Edinburgh to London – 500 miles in seven days, including seventeen hours on a bike one day and an open water swim across Lake Windermere another. Davina, you are my hero and the most fun company ever – but seriously? I couldn't have done any of that at twenty, never mind fifty. No wonder it was so easy to compare myself and come up wanting.

'Your trouble is you have always done everything so late that you think you are ten years younger than you are,' said my all-knowing brother, Matthew.

It's another valid point – and maybe having such a young family gave me an almost 'fake' forties, when I was living the life of a young mum, adored by wide-eyed toddlers rather than mocked by sneering teenagers for being 'SO embarrassing'. Although I was horribly aware of my age at the mummy and toddler groups – not helped when Billy announced one day, 'You're the oldest mummy here at music club! I checked. I know I shouldn't show off, but I've told everyone!'

Of course he was really proud – when you are three being older is the best thing ever. Not so much for me!

'Great,' I said with a grimace.

Still, it kept me young and vigorous.

But now I'm suddenly very aware of being middle aged. Within days of realising that I was going to be fifty at my next birthday – and by that I mean properly registering it – I started to notice that the skin on my arms was looking papery. It really was perplexing. Where had it come from, this new, old skin tone? Clearly it hadn't arrived overnight, and yet I'd only just noticed it. Was it because my hormones were reconfiguring, or because I was more conscious of ageing?

After that, an image kept popping into my mind of sitting between my mother and grandmother in the car on the way to Dyfed in Wales, where we went on holiday every year when I was young. During the long hours of the journey, I used to compare my hands with theirs, fascinated by how similar they were in shape and yet different in terms of age. It was like having our family connection laid bare before me, connected yet separated by the generations. Mine were classic kid's hands, with nails either broken or sensibly short, covered in scrapes, bruises and scratches from play and play-fights. My mum's were the epitome of elegance: smoothly moisturised, with long, slim fingers and perfectly polished nails. My grandma's nails were also perfectly polished, but her hands – understandably – were blemished by age, the skin wrinkled and crêpey. Now, as I looked at my own hands, it seemed that they had become like my grandma's, and I hadn't even noticed when they were like my mum's! Presumably, at some point, buffed and polished for the red carpet, they must have looked perfect, like hers, but I'd missed it.

But isn't that the trouble with midlife? It feels as though you only notice your peak when you have passed it. You remember just how hot the sun was at its highest when it is on its way down and the shadows have started to creep across the lawn.

And, oh, those shadows. The spectres of loss. As I turned to look ahead to what the next few decades might hold, it all seemed to be about loss. Loss of looks, loss of health, loss of sense and senses, loss of loved ones, loss of purpose and usefulness.

'It's all so depressing,' I groaned. 'No wonder we midlifers end up asking, "Is it all downhill from here?"'

'Kate Garraway, get a grip,' said Anne, my friend from school. 'Your trouble is you don't know how lucky you are to be worrying about turning fifty. A lot of people don't get the chance, you know.'

A tidal wave of guilt and shame swept over me. Anne, a nurse who runs a unit at a hospital in Oxford, knows all too well how cruel fate can be. As do I – and I thought guiltily about my friend, Jane, who was killed at twenty-seven by a drunk driver, just as she was coming home from celebrating getting her first job as a junior doctor. I also think of my friend, Kara, who at thirty-six, after years of heartbreak, finally found a wonderful man and began trying to have a family with him, only to have her dreams of becoming a mum – along with her life – snatched from her by the silent killer, ovarian cancer.

But knowing that others are far worse off than you, and being grateful for your own good luck, sometimes isn't enough. Their bad luck seems only to emphasise how cruel life can be and what misery might be around the corner for you.

Still, Anne was right – I needed to get a grip.

If old age was hurtling towards me at a rate of knots, I owed it to the ones who never got the chance to moan about midlife to take on the challenge of loving it. The goal was to learn how to be amazing at fifty and beyond, to feel so fabulous and excited about the rest of my life that if someone gave me three wishes, and one was to go back in time I would say, 'You know what? No.'

I wanted every day to be better than the last. I decided that if Mother Nature was going to take away my youth, I was going to find something better to replace it. It was a revolution. I was going to overthrow the doom and gloom of middle age and transform myself into a state of joy, vitality and wisdom.

So where do you start when you realise you need a total mind, body and soul transformation?

I started with the one thing I knew deep down was the most superficial, the one thing our mums tell us is really not important at all.

I started with the way I looked. Obviously.

CHAPTER 3

The Facelift Dilemma

It's not as though I have ever been what my granddad would call 'a real looker'. You know the sort – the ones who are born with naturally perfect features and bodies that can stop traffic and turn the opposite sex into gibbering wrecks. I have often wondered what it must be like to be one of those people, to be someone who doesn't have to really worry about saying something actually interesting, because whatever nonsense spills forth, people will always be keen to hear it, just because they are so chuffed to be looking at you and talking to you. Life must be so much easier.

I, though, have always had to work on 'personality'.

I remember once in drama club at college, we all had to sit in a circle and say something positive about another member of the group's appearance. I got John, a totally gorgeous blond hunk of a lad I had secretly fancied for three terms. He paused for what seemed like an age and stared at me with a furrowed brow. My heart leapt. Maybe he was struggling to single out just one of the myriad things he adored about me, I thought. Perhaps he was hesitating in case he praised my charms so warmly that everyone would realise he was secretly in love with me. No such luck.

Instead, he finally announced, 'If I was lost and didn't know where to go and I saw your face, you would definitely be the person I would turn to for help.'

'Oh yes, that's so true! Yes, that's Kate,' agreed the rest of the group.

Great. He saw me as reassuring, safe and practical, then. Like a comforting maiden aunt or a living satnav – not the sexy siren I was hoping for.

But it could have been worse. At least I didn't actively repel people – and over the years, with a good haircut, a full face of make-up and the right lighting, I had learnt to make myself look pretty good. Or, at least, the best I could.

But now it felt as though Mother Nature was about to chip all that away – and nothing could turn back time. Or could it?

Arguably, one of the advantages of ageing in 2017 is that 'we have the technology', as they used to say in the opening sequence of *The Six Million Dollar Man*. OK, so nothing is going to ACTUALLY turn back time, but I might be able to erase its effects superficially. Facelifts can stretch skin, fillers can plump up hollowed cheeks and Botox can freeze frown lines. But just because cosmetic surgery is there, should we do it? I started to think maybe I should and would.

'I want a facelift,' I said to my husband one night, as I cleared away the kids' leftover fish fingers.

'Don't be ridiculous,' he said. 'People with facelifts look weird.'

'Ah, they're the ones you notice,' I said. 'You spot them because they're not very good.'

I began to reel off a list of stars that I knew for absolute certain had had facelifts. Or, at least, I'd heard as much from the friend of a make-up artist who once powdered them on set, and they said it was true – which was good enough for me (but apparently not for my lawyers, which is why I can't put their names in this book!).

'OK,' he said. 'So they look good now, but what about in five or ten years' time, when it all slips? What do you do then? Have another one? Seek out increasingly drastic and weird ways to fight time? Where will it all end? And anyway, I love your laughter lines.'

Look, I loved my laughter lines, too. It was the misery lines I hated – the increasingly deep grooves that ran from my nose to my mouth, making me look all droopy and sad. The furrows between my eyebrows that were starting to be my 'resting face' and made me look furious even when I wasn't. And the jowls – oh those jowls! When I looked in the mirror first thing in the morning, they made me look like I'd already had the worst day ever, even before it had started.

Over the next few days I found myself increasingly 'trying out' how a facelift would improve me by pulling my skin up from under my chin and back from behind my ears. Instantly, I looked like what I thought was the real me, by which I meant the younger me. But also somehow the happier me – the face I wanted to present to the world. After all, who wants to wake up in the morning and see a miserable old crow on the telly? Didn't someone once say, 'Smile, and the world smiles with you'?

Soon my kids started to notice something was up. 'Why do you keep doing that with your face?' my seven-year-old, Billy, asked when we were stuck at traffic lights and I was at it again in the rear-view mirror.

'Your mum wants a facelift,' Derek said.

Billy looked terrified. 'What's a facelift?' I guess he was imagining some kind of creepy science fiction face transplant – which I guess in a way it is.

'It's just a little operation,' I said, glowering at Derek, as if it were his fault I had been caught out.

I felt embarrassed that I was exposing my gorgeous little seven-year-old to my midlife woes. This is not great role modelling or parenting, I thought to myself.

I'm supposed to be teaching him that appearances aren't important.

But he wasn't to be quietened. 'What does it do?' he asked.

'It just pulls your skin tighter here, and here,' I said, giving a quick demonstration.

He was horrified. 'Don't do that!' He seemed really upset. 'You wouldn't look like my mum!'

'Whatever I look like, I will always be your mum,' I said, hugging him. 'Anyway, what DOES your mum look like?'

'Comfy. Mum, you are the comfiest, cosiest person in the world.'

My heart melted. Because of course, as a mum, that's exactly what you want to be – comfy. But as a wife? As a lover? As a thrusting, go-getting employee? I wasn't so sure.

It turned out my husband and son weren't the only ones appalled that I was considering cosmetic surgery.

'You can't!' screeched Ranvir Singh, my friend and co-presenter on *Good Morning Britain*. Ranvir is always so gentle and supportive that the ferocity of her response actually made me jump in my chair. 'I have rarely felt so strongly about anything,' she went on. 'You forget that before I worked with you I watched you on the telly as I was growing up. And the thing I loved most about you was the fact you were so real. You're not a perfectly pretty, painted presenter. You are normal and down to earth. You laugh at yourself and don't take yourself too seriously. When I used to watch you on TV, I felt you were just like me. If you have a facelift, you will be fake and destroy everything I adore about you. I would feel betrayed.'

Blimey.

Fiona Phillips, my TV presenter and *Mirror* columnist mate, went even further. 'Please don't! It's not just that I think you don't need it, it's that I think this increasing obsession with cosmetic surgery generally is damaging to women. I would never have Botox or fillers, because women aren't meant to look wrinkle-free as they get older. Nor should they be expected to. And it's so unfair that some women can afford to trick Mother Nature and others can't. We are going to end up with two tiers in our society, if we are not careful – the half who can afford it and the others who can't. It'll be like a new class system. It just doesn't seem right.'

Blimey again.

Now I felt I was letting down the sisterhood. I could have argued in return that life is unfair – a visit to any accident and emergency department will remind you of that. I could have said that relying on the luck of good genes was also unfair. Fiona has been blessed with her mum's great cheekbones, a lovely complexion and a figure that would make a sixteen-year-old look saggy in comparison. What if someone wasn't so lucky? What if they hadn't had the support and education to look after themselves in the first half of their life, nor the time to keep fit or the luck of good health? If, at fifty, they wanted to buy themselves a bit of Botox, instead of a holiday, because it made them feel better, who would begrudge them that?

I could have said all this, but I didn't. I respected my friends' attitudes to ageing and thought it best, for once, to keep quiet.

I guess I am used to people taking a 'position' on the way I look – it happens a lot when you are on TV. I have never minded people who've seen me on the telly coming up to me and chatting. I rather like it, actually. It's friendly. Maybe it's because I grew up in a small town where my parents knew or had connections with most people, so when I was out with them as a child, someone would always stop and say hello. Being recognised feels like an extension of that. It also makes the job rewarding when you realise you are connecting with people who are watching and they 'get' what you do. But it does surprise me how outspoken people can be – a lot more outspoken, I suspect, than they would be with their actual friends and family.

'Ooh, you look so much slimmer in real life. You look massive on the telly!'

Er, thanks?!

Or, 'Your hair doesn't look nearly as bad in real life. It's actually quite shiny.'

Oh, OK!

I remember when, during my maternity leave with Darcey, I let my highlights 'go' because I was so busy – and ended up with so much root that I thought I might as well dye the rest of it back closer to my natural colour. So, when I returned to *GMTV*, I was no longer a blonde, but a brunette.

Well, you would have thought I had punched somebody's mum in the face. People started phoning and writing in (it was the days before the prevalence of social media – remember those?) saying, 'What has she DONE?', 'It looks AWFUL', 'Why would she do that to herself?'.

There was the kind of outrage from some people that I imagine I will feel the first time my daughter Darcey comes home as a teenager, having chopped off her long, beautiful, reddish-brown hair that I adore – and dyed it black. There was a feeling that somehow my hair was their property. It's flattering in a way because it shows people feel connected to you, which is what you want as a presenter, but it's also rather unnerving.

Of course, the camera itself is often your harshest critic. The new hi-def ones really accentuate every detail, as I discovered the day I was trying out a new mascara with extra 'filaments' to make my lashes look longer. Following the instructions, I applied a gluey substance to my lashes from one bottle and then covered them with tiny filaments from another bottle that stuck and built up layers so the lashes looked longer. Well, I had obviously got the technique wrong, because bits of the little filaments started dropping on to my cheeks. They were tiny black flecks, which would be barely noticeable if I was sitting in front of you. But under the scrutiny of the lens they must have looked massive, because people started tweeting and emailing. 'What is wrong with Kate's face?', 'Has she not even bothered to look in a mirror this morning?', 'How rude, how messy!' and so on.

It got to the point where my co-presenter, Ben Shephard, said, 'Can you sort out your mascara, please? We are talking about big world issues on the show today and everybody is obsessing about your mascara. It's very distracting!'

So I am used to all of that – but my friends who know me off camera would never usually comment about my appearance. Until, that is, a load of them started to turn fifty, at which point ageing became a hot topic and suddenly everyone felt the urge to chip in and have a view.

I noticed it when I went to two fiftieth birthday parties in a month, both of them full of friends who weren't connected with TV, many of whom hadn't seen each other for nearly twenty years. Both times, as the evening wore on, we peeled off into groups and there was the inevitable discussion about 'who hasn't aged well'. That is, who looked wrinkled, had got fat or was losing their hair. No one wanted to be in that category. But there were also debates about who'd had a 'nip and tuck' or hair plugs, and no one wanted to be in that group, either. You couldn't win, really; you were judged if you looked old and judged if you had done something to stop looking old.

Bad enough to be getting older at all, I thought. At least let's be allowed to handle it in our own way.

I was still feeling torn about whether to try cosmetic surgery, so I turned for advice to the woman who has been like the big sister I never had, my friend Penny. When I first met Penny Stokes-Hilton at a mate's house, she said I looked like a bird that had flown into a window, all broken and tragic. And I guess, in a way, I was. My first marriage had just ended and I was heartbroken. My confidence had been destroyed, I was doubting myself and the world around me and felt consumed with my own sadness. I looked a wreck, too.

I had never been particularly good at girly grooming. Even in my twenties, while my mates were splashing out on mani-pedis on Saturday mornings, I would rather lie in bed with my nose in a book and join them for the gossip and cake afterwards. But now my grooming had gone from haphazard to serious neglect.

Penny immediately scooped me up and, along with her younger sister Vickie, began to rescue and rebuild me. They were the epitome of girly glamour, with polished nails and bouffed, blowdried hair, the sort of women who, even when they were single, were always perfectly bikini-waxed. They were the types who applied body moisturiser every day to make their skin feel silky smooth to the touch, even if they were the only ones who were going to be seeing and feeling it. I, however, was the epitome of neglect, with eyebrows bushier than Noel Gallagher, unshaven legs and hedge-backwards hair, among other signs of dishevelment.

They stripped me down – literally, on one occasion, to apply all-over fake tan, the first time I had tried it; their crimson-taloned hands rubbing lotion all over my body until I looked like I had been dipped in gravy browning. They introduced me to the Hollywood bikini wax – the first time was so painful that I only managed one half, so I was Bolivian jungle one side, Hollywood the other. It was two weeks before I was brave enough to go back and have the whole thing done properly. And all the while they were making over my outside, they were pouring out love and support to build up my inside. 'You are gorgeous. Oh my God, look at you! If that ex-husband could see you now ...'

'You have to make looking good part of your routine,' they would lecture me. 'It's not just about being attractive. It says to the world, "I care about myself," and it follows that if you care, then the world will care about you, too.'

It was good advice.

Eight years ago, as Penny approached her fiftieth, she took the next step from plucking and waxing to surgery. I didn't get why, then – she looked great to me – but now, as I approached fifty, I was beginning to understand.

'I wanted to do everything I could to show my best face to the world,' she told me. 'To ready myself for the rest of my life and whatever it was going to bring. My life was better than it had ever been, but I'd started to hate the way I looked in photographs. I didn't look like what I felt was the real me.'

After years of heartbreak and broken marriages, she had finally found a man she adored, remarried, reinvented herself and was feeling happy again. She just didn't want her worn-out face to be the face people saw.

And, for her, it worked.

Seeing a younger face in the mirror made her FEEL younger. She suddenly seemed to have more energy, started eating better and living more healthily and happily. It was as if she had played a psychological trick on herself. Looking younger made her act younger, too.

But of course there are downsides, not least the cost. A good plastic surgeon (and you certainly don't want to go to a bad one) will charge upwards of ten thousand pounds. Hard to justify, even if you have the money – and having just moved house, we'd had to avoid any spending splurges for a while, let alone a big one like this. So if I went and spent money we didn't have on a facelift, how selfish and unfair would it be?

Then there is the recovery. Penny was up and about after two weeks and had minimal bruising and swelling. However, the average recovery is a month and it can take longer, she warned me. She was lucky, but residual swelling and bruises are common for up to a year after going under the knife – and some patients end up with long-term numbness in their cheeks or behind their ears, while others experience frequent twinges of pain. 'You have to be prepared for post-operative complications,' she said. 'You have to feel it's worth it.'

Mmm, I wasn't sure it was. As a working mum with two young children, could I justify taking to my bed for three weeks? Neglecting them and putting more pressure on my husband? I would feel guilty enough if it was an operation for a medical emergency, but for this? I knew what my mum would say: 'You've gone bonkers! This is midlife madness and needless vanity.'

Yet, all around me, people were succumbing to this 'madness' – and they weren't just midlifers either. One presenter I know confessed she'd been having 'mini-lifts' and Botox for years.

'I have a little "procedure" every six months,' she said. 'It fractionally tightens the skin – it is virtually unnoticeable – but it means that my face never starts to drop. It keeps everything in place, so that I don't have to do anything dramatic later on, and avoids that "lizard" look, when you pull everything up and back at once and look like you have been through a wind tunnel.'

She is thirty-two and has been doing this for six years.

It wasn't just women in front of camera, either. While I was having my make-up done for a BBC show a couple of years ago, I was moaning about my jowls and bags (as usual!) and the make-up artist, who was in her early thirties, said breezily, 'Oh, I've had fillers for years and I also have something called "threading" done.'

'Threading, what's that?'

'It's a bit scary,' she said. 'The surgeon literally sews threads under your skin and pulls them tight to lift your face up. But they are invisible to the eye and dissolve after a few weeks – and, hey presto, you look firmer than ever.'

I couldn't believe that she had said it so matter-of-factly, with no embarrassment whatsoever, as if she were talking about a new shade of lipstick.

It got me thinking that maybe, in the future, cosmetic procedures will become much more accepted, even the norm. I thought about how, when my mum was younger, dyeing your hair was something you didn't advertise. It was seen as racy, a bit cheap, and definitely cheating. So even now, when my mum goes to the hairdresser (often with me), she'll tell my dad, 'I'm just off for my special conditioning treatment, darling.'

She likes to keep as her little secret that she is dyeing her hair to cover the grey, whereas among my friends everyone openly bleaches and dyes, not just to cover grey but to generally enhance the way they look. It's just a useful tool for looking better, and maybe that's the way the next generation will regard cosmetic surgery.

'It's already like that over here,' my friend Carla Romano told me. Carla was the Los Angeles correspondent at *GMTV* for many years and has now settled down with her American husband and two-year-old daughter in that famously glamorous zip code, Beverly Hills 90210. Despite remaining a down-to-earth Scot herself, she is surrounded by people who have 'fillers and Botox as openly as going to the dentist'.

'People think you are odd if you *don't* do it,' she says. 'Whenever I shop on Rodeo Drive, where all the designer stores are (do you remember it from the film *Pretty Woman*?), all the cafés around there are full of people eating salad while holding ice packs to their faces to reduce the swelling after one procedure or another.

Nobody bats an eyelid. And I am not talking about the film stars either, just ordinary souls, like you and me.

'I do loads of stuff that I would have been laughed out of town for back home in Glasgow. I've had diamond facials and a gold leaf facial. I even had a placenta facial the other day. Sounds disgusting, but it was actually very relaxing. God knows whose placenta it was, but it seemed to do the trick.'

The way Carla described it made me feel less like I was cheating if I had cosmetic enhancement and more like I was letting myself down by not trying it. Was I missing out on what the modern world had to offer? Just as I had twenty years ago, when I had wondered why so many girls had golden, tanned legs through even the worst of the British summers – and eventually discovered that the answer was fake tan.

Armed with Carla's enthusiasm and a list of the least scary of the current trendy treatments, I decided to stop talking and start trying out a few anti-ageing tricks.

First I had a Computer Aided Cosmetology Instrument (CACI) treatment – two probes with electric currents running through them, which make the muscles in your jaw and cheeks twitch. CACI is supposed to strengthen your facial muscles and so lift everything up; it's a kind of workout for the face. It made my fillings jangle, which I didn't like, but after a course of ten treatments I felt I saw an improvement. Although, just like going to the gym, you would have to keep it up to ensure long-term results.

I saw a doctor in Mayfair whose consulting room was full of strange-looking equipment with levers and buttons everywhere. 'It's like the deck of the TARDIS in here,' I joked. 'Are you Doctor Who?'

She'd clearly heard that one before. 'If you're asking whether I can take you back in time, I can certainly try,' she said dryly.

I spent an hour under a 'red lamp', which was supposed to 'reignite the collagen in my skin on a cellular level'. It felt nice, like sunbathing. Then she smothered my skin in super-rich, vitamin-packed goo and rolled a tool covered in tiny needles over my face, making tiny punctures that would let in all those youth-promoting ingredients. Afterwards my skin glowed.

In Soho I had something called a 'soft peel', which is basically a chemical face peel for wimps. They leave the chemicals on your skin just for a few seconds before they wipe them off, to avoid burning. Afterwards my skin was so taut that it almost looked shiny, in a good way. But I had to wear full sunblock for weeks afterwards because my complexion was ultra sensitive to sun damage, so I couldn't help wondering if I was exposing myself to more potential age deterioration from the sun than I was curing, especially if I went back for regular treatments.

I took advice on Botox. One surgeon said it was the greatest thing ever, not just for freeing the skin of wrinkles, but for your whole well-being. 'There's an argument to say that having Botox makes you feel happier, because it stops you frowning,' he said.

He cited a 2009 study of a small group of women by psychologists at the University of Cardiff, in which the women taking part who were given Botox reported being happier and less anxious than the control group who hadn't. According to the study, it wasn't because they felt unlined and more attractive, it was because they had stopped frowning. In the same year, a study in Munich found that people who'd had Botox experienced a weaker emotional response in their brains than those who hadn't had it when they were asked to make angry faces. It works the other way too, the studies say; so if you frown while you're removing a splinter, you may well feel more pain than if you keep your expression neutral.

Amazing. So Botox not only makes you look younger, but feel happier too.

'But with your tiny forehead, you probably shouldn't go near it,' another surgeon warned. 'Your brow is already low set and Botox could make it even worse. If you do have it done, it would need to be administered by an absolute expert.' (For expert, read: expensive.) 'And it would have to be very small, very subtle amounts, done more frequently than most,' she said. (For subtle and frequent, read: even more expensive.)

I began to think that this was all rather bewildering, time-consuming and costly. Although it was nice that people were commenting on how good my skin was looking, the improvement was actually making me feel more conscious of the way I looked and how age was affecting me. And it was making me scrutinise others in a way I hadn't before. I wasn't sure I liked it.

I'm thinking about the time I interviewed Nicole Kidman. I was well aware of the rumours about her having all sorts of cosmetic enhancements since the last time I had met her, so I was curious to see what she looked like up close. I sat a foot away from her and in all honesty she looked genuinely and naturally youthful and blooming – seriously, I've seen crêpier skin on a baby. While she chattered away about her new movie, I found myself so distracted by the flawlessness of her skin that at one point I blurted out, 'What moisturiser do you use?'

She stopped and looked at me, confused. I couldn't blame her. The movie was about highbrow themes like love and loss, survival and the triumph of the human spirit. Skincare was not an obvious line of questioning.

She clearly thought I was an idiot, but was too polite to say. Or perhaps she could tell that my question was a plea, woman to woman, to lead me to the secret fountain of youth, which she had clearly discovered several decades before, because she generously ventured, 'Clarins!' with a beaming smile. 'I've used it for years.'

I instantly made a note to go out and buy some. But I suspect that Nicole, being very fair-skinned, was probably wearing a big hat and sitting under a huge parasol for all those years while I was slapping on cheap tanning oil and offering myself up to the great, glorious wrinkle-maker in the sky. Or that might be part of the disparity between us.

Either way it was embarrassing and, glorious as her skin was, I really had to get a grip.

The next morning, Lisa Mejuto, one of *Good Morning Britain*'s make-up artists, told me some hard truths. 'We see it all in the make-up chair, you know – the telltale puckering that shows the nip here, the over-taut skin that shows the tuck there. I can tell you honestly that real sex appeal and beauty come from the power you have within you rather than from anything external, however well it's done. So why don't you leave the outside to us? After all, we've been turning sows' ears into silk purses for years.' She laughed, then continued:

'You should really just focus on your inside and get your head around ageing. That's where the real power of a woman's attractiveness and sexiness lies.'

She had a point. Before I spent another penny, I had some digging to do. And a few secrets to reveal, too.

CHAPTER 4

Tricks of the Trade: Smoke and Mirrors

You are probably thinking that it's about time I got stuck into the nitty-gritty and started tackling the really important scary stuff that comes with the ageing process. I did assure you at the start that if you came along with me, I would share some of the deeper insights my adventure into learning to love the rest of my life has uncovered.

And I will, I promise. But because I also think there is a strong link between feeling good about getting older and making the best of your appearance, before we really get under the skin of things (bad pun absolutely intended!) I am going to first reveal the tricks of the trade that I have always benefited from because of my job – it seems only fair after all! Then you too can shine as we travel through this midlife wilderness together and emerge triumphant.

The lovely actress Linda Gray, famous for her role in the US TV series *Dallas* and more recently in the British soap *Hollyoaks*, looks spectacular for her seventy-six years. She told me recently that she has good face days and bad face days. 'The good days are a blessing – and on the bad days I rely on the magic of a talented make-up artist.'

Well, if it's good enough for Sue Ellen ...!

I didn't really need convincing by Linda, though. Joanna Lumley had already won me over. Years ago, I was sitting in the make-up room at *GMTV* when Joanna Lumley sat down in the chair next to me, because she was going to be a guest on the show.

'What would you like today?' asked the make-up artist, putting a gown around her neck to protect her clothes.

'I don't care what you do, just make me absolutely fabulous,' Joanna Lumley replied.

Considering the show she was most famous for, I thought this was typically hilarious of her – and also rather a brilliant approach to the wonderful transformation that takes place in TV make-up rooms.

These make-up artists really are magicians – and they have such a bewildering array of products and tools that it can be a bit overwhelming. When I first started,

I used to say, 'Oh, just use a bit of brown eyeshadow please, don't go over the top.'

But I soon realised that I was missing out on all their skilled little illusions – the magical smoke and mirrors they employ to fool people into thinking you look better than you do. So now when I plop down in the make-up chair with my pile of briefs and laptop to prepare for *Good Morning Britain*, I say, 'Do what you like. I'll be wearing red. Just make me look absolutely fabulous.'

My job has a lot of perks, and one of them is being surrounded by this team of absolute wizards, who transform me from the mess I look like when I arrive at the studio at three in the morning to what you see when I go on-air at six. Most days, it's quite a speedy process, because there isn't much time after we've had our editorial meeting and prepared for our interviews in the newsroom. They do what they can in twenty minutes or half an hour. However, the entire box of tricks comes out for red carpet events. These are always fun, because a load of ITV presenters get together at the ITV studio make-up and dressing rooms beforehand and it's got the atmosphere of a gang of girls getting ready for a big night out. Susanna and I love it, because neither of us have sisters, so we think this is what it must be like – swapping clothes and make-up. In fact, Susanna has always been very sisterly to me, and she is always there to lean on if I need her. Isn't that the great thing about friendships in midlife? Everyone wanders about in their dressing gowns, washing their hair in the make-up room sinks and having a good gossip. There's masses of excitement and anticipation in the air. 'Help! What should I do with my hair that's different?'

There is quite a lot of anxiety around red carpet events. You're feverishly excited about having the chance to go to a swanky premiere or party, but you also know that people will be scrutinising you. The magazines do big spreads where you get a tick or a cross and you feel quite exposed, because rather than being comfortable in your normal clothes, you've suddenly got chunks of flesh on display that you normally wouldn't even show to your cat.

Everyone has their paranoias. And we all chip in, swap handbags and jewellery, and offer lots of support when one or another is having doubts about their frock.

'Wow, you look amazing!'

'Aw, I think I look a bit booby.'

'I don't like my bra.'

'Can someone sew some sleeves on this dress to cover my arms, please?'

The ITV Gala is a really fun event. At the same time, the pressure is on, because all the great and good are there – the bosses and sponsors. You want to show people you've still got it and can hold your own among the younger stars. The cameras flash wildly as you arrive.

Last time I went, I sat down in the make-up chair beforehand and said not just my usual 'absolutely fabulous' but also, 'I'd like you to make me look young, please.'

'These are hands, not wands,' said Lisa, my wise make-up artist, with a giggle. When she realised I wasn't joking, she said, 'Oh, OK, I'll give it my best shot.'

'But, really – if you looked at the rest of my life as a walk along the red carpet, how would you go about making me look the best I possibly can?' I asked.

The room was buzzing and people kept chipping in on each other's conversations.

'Looking young is all about the skin,' said Helen Hand, who has made up everyone from Sienna Miller to Honor Blackman, and several prime ministers into the bargain. 'Priming and prepping your complexion is essential. Do a full cleanse, tone and moisturise at night. In the morning, splash your face with cold water and use an SPF day cream. Treat yourself to a facial every now and then. Massage oils into your face at night – Trilogy's rosehip oil is lovely.'

I touched my cheek nervously. Helen didn't need to remind me of the importance of young-looking skin. A few days earlier, Susanna Reid and I had been given age spots, wrinkles and grey wigs by a team of prosthetics experts as part of a new *Good Morning Britain* campaign to highlight loneliness in older people, called 1 Million Minutes. The idea was to age us forty years – and the results were transformative. It was very strange looking in the mirror, like seeing into the future, and it really made me appreciate how I look and feel now.

'If you spend money on anything, spend it on your foundation,' Helen added. 'Go for something with a gleam. You definitely have to experiment before you find the right brand for you. Play around like you did as a teenager. Go to a department store counter and try out different products – there will be something that suits you individually. Then walk out into the street and check it in daylight, because the lighting in shops is totally different.'

This is very good advice. Another place to look is in the rear-view mirror of a car, which gives you the cruellest of reflections, so if you look OK there then you are fine. Still, it's important to remember that nobody really sees you like that, because rear-view mirrors are magnified and weirdly distorting, so don't worry, it's never that bad!

'Don't be afraid to ask for make-up and skincare samples at the counters,' Helen said. 'We're talking about expensive products, so you don't want to make mistakes. If they've run out of sample tubes and sachets, you should be able to take away a small amount of the tester product in a container – just buy a small travel pot from a chemist and take it in with you.'

That seems fair enough. Then you can go home and play around to see which ones work the best.

There's a temptation to use more make-up as you get older, but I actually think that less foundation is the way to go. Heavier make-up tends to look cakey – it clings and emphasises wrinkles and cracks, as my daughter, Darcey, is always pointing out. She can't bear to see me made up for TV. 'Why are you wearing that horrible stuff?' she says. 'It sticks in your creases and makes you look old, Mum.'

Charming! She's right, though – and she doesn't comment when I'm wearing light foundation, because she doesn't think I'm wearing make-up at all.

I look for foundation products that are barely there and use them sparingly, keeping it light around my eyes and going slightly stronger on my cheeks and chin, where I have broken thread veins. Laura Mercier and Chanel both do fantastic light foundations, and Bourjois and Boots No. 7 do cheaper but very good versions, according to Helen Hand. They don't cover all the freckles and little blemishes, but actually that's quite a youthful thing, because it makes your skin look real, while still evening out its tone. At the moment I'm using a colour correcting cream by Stila. Rather disconcertingly, it comes out green, but adjusts to your skin tone and covers the flaws, even when it dries. Then I apply loads of blusher.

For me, the key is to put health and definition back into your face. So when you get older, you might have more of a sallow complexion. Perhaps you're tired or not very well. That's when blusher is your friend, because you don't want to have a flat, monotone face. I think a slightly pink or light peachy shade is best for white skin, but everyone is different. Darker skin tones can take much warmer, richer shades like claret red or terracotta.

'Go for the colour you see when you pinch your cheek,' Helen suggested.

'And don't worry about Kim Kardashian-style contouring,' Lisa added. 'It looks totally over the top in real life.'

'When you get to a certain age, make-up is less about trendiness than making the most of the features you've got,' Helen agreed. 'So if your lips have shrunk, really go for the eyes, and vice versa. If you have skinny lips, don't draw attention to them – just use a light gloss.' By now, all the make-up team was joining in, Heather and Teri too.

'Lining your lips is a really good idea,' Suzy chipped in from across the room. 'Play around and find a lip liner that's really close to your lip skin tone. It's not about darkening your lips, it's about making the edges really solid to stop the lipstick "bleeding" – that's when it runs into the fine lines around your mouth. You can also use a reflective concealer like Touche Éclat very close to the skin around the lips, especially on the top lip. It makes your mouth look fuller and again helps to prevent your lipstick bleeding.'

This is a great tip. I don't put foundation on my top lip any more because I've got so many fine lines, and reflective concealer works much better.

'You can spend less money on things like eyeshadow,' Suzy said. 'Just avoid anything with a frosty sheen, because it can stick in the lines on your upper lids.

'Most people's eyes tend to droop a little bit in their forties and if you just put colour on your lids, it's not going to do the trick,' she went on. 'Generally you need to apply a dark, neutralising, warm brown to your brow bone to open your eyes up.'

'Fantastic,' I said. 'Anything else?'

'Refresh your make-up,' Lisa said. 'If you don't, you look out of date.'

'Really? But who is going to notice?'

'It's not about having the exact shade of pinky red blush that's fresh off the catwalks,' she said, 'but when you do something new with your appearance, however subtle, people often comment on how nice you're looking without knowing why you appear different. No one consciously notices – it's subliminal – but freshening your look somehow makes you seem connected.'

She's totally right, of course. Just the hint of a modern twist adds freshness and youthfulness.

'Eyebrows can take ten years off you,' Helen said. 'If you have them done well, it's almost like having a facelift.' Helen has made up Brooke Shields – now there's someone with serious eyebrows. Brooke loved Helen because she got her eyebrows: she brushed them upwards and they looked fabulous.

Hi-def eyebrows are the way forward. HD eyebrow shaping involves tinting the fluffy bits – your natural hair – above your eyebrow line and then removing the hair underneath. It gives you a great shape, has a lifting effect and opens up your eyes. Just make sure you don't end up with what's unfairly known as 'the Scouse brow', which is too pencilled in and looks like a big black slug.

'Eyelashes make a big difference, too,' said Mel, *GMB*'s young and funky make-up artist. 'Your lashes tend to thin out and fade in colour as you get older and one trick is to smudge something dark right at the root of the lashes. This could be a hard line and a flick, if it suits you, or just a dab of soft, dark eyeshadow. Curling your lashes is really important, because that lifts and opens the eyes. I do it every day.'

Having eyelash extensions is fantastic but can weaken the existing lashes, so it's not a long-term solution. False eyelashes are good, but a bit of a pain to stick on and get off. Suzy recommended using an eyelash growth serum that thickens lashes. I was already tempted to get some because it had transformed my friend, Julia. After three months of painting it on her eyelids every night, her eyelashes were suddenly long, thick and luscious again, like they used to be in her twenties.

Eyelash serum is a fantastic product if your eyelashes are thinning, or if you've had alopecia or lost your hair through chemotherapy. It works on eyebrows too and you can buy it in high street chemists. 'It's a bit pricey, but lasts forever,' Julia told me, adding that she'd noticed a difference within three weeks of using it.

By now, Lisa had done quite a bit of magic to make me look younger, despite having implied I was a lost cause. I was happy with my face. Next, for a few conjuring tricks from my two hairdressers, Paul Haskell and Pauline Simmons.

These two have worked absolute wonders. I've had issues with my hair all my life because I've always had loads of it. When I was at school it was just enormous – I looked like Crystal Tipps from the children's cartoon. In the days before straightening irons, anti-frizz shampoo and argan oil, there wasn't a lot I could do with it, either. But I'm thankful for it now that I have had expert help to tame it, even though Ben Shephard says, 'Working with you is like working with an Afghan hound! You shed hair everywhere.'

First I asked Paul Haskell for advice on keeping older hair looking good. Paul has worked his magic on Jayne Torvill's hair for years, along with a host of other stars, including Bruno Tonioli.

'As you get older, the condition of your hair deteriorates,' he said. 'It gets thinner, drier and rougher. But there are lots of great products around that can fake shine and condition – and the glossier and shinier your hair, the younger you look. There's a fantastic range of shine sprays and oils. I particularly like Redken Shine Flash. It's also worth spending the money on more expensive shampoos and conditioners: the Oribe range is pretty fabulous, although very expensive. Every time you use it, though, your hair gets better and better – so maybe you could have it as a special Christmas or birthday present, and use it sparingly.'

To his advice I would add that, because my hair is so coarse (like a horse's mane!), I swear by putting Moroccan oil on the hair while it is still damp and blowdrying it in. Using hair serums when your hair is wet works wonders for smoothing too, but if your hair is very fine, don't overdo it or it will go limp.

'What about the colour? Should we all go blonde when the grey starts?' I asked Pauline Simmons, who has done pretty much everyone's hair, and has worked on big shows like the MTV music awards and the BAFTAs too.

'People used to say that you can never be too blonde, but actually going too dark or too light can be really ageing,' she said. 'It's much more flattering to try new ways of covering the grey. Dip dye and ombré are very trendy. With dip dye you have dark roots and light ends, whereas ombré is about gradual blending from dark roots to light ends with the lengths somewhere in between. Don't go for the extreme version – leave that to the twentysomethings. Talk to your hairdresser about doing it subtly or try a method hairdressers call "balayage", not using traditional foils as with highlights and lowlights, but putting them in kind of freestyle, not in regimented rows. It will make you look up to date, and be softer and more flattering. Don't be afraid of a block colour to cover grey, but make sure it's not matte. Go for a dye that will keep the shine.'

Paul developed a highlighting style for me that he called 'fashion-forward face-framing flashes'. What can I say, celebrity hairdressers love their fancy names! Because I am naturally brunette (did you guess?!), he said I should keep as much of my natural colour as possible, but have blonde 'flashes' around the face to brighten everything up and keep it soft next to my skin.

It involved putting foils into my hair in a kind of halo around my face, through the sides and fringe. When he first took them out, I wasn't sure – it kind of looked like I had fallen face forward into a custard pie, like a spiky lion's mane of blonde. But after it was washed out and blowdried, it did indeed look 'fashion forward' and I loved it! So it's always worth trying something new.

When it comes to your haircut, Paul says the general rules for an age-flattering style are that you should go for some height at the crown and some softness in the style. Really hard, short haircuts are going to be harsh on the face and probably best left to flawless, gamine-featured seventeen-year-olds.

'Don't go to the other extreme, though,' Pauline warned. 'People make the mistake of having no "strength" in their haircut and the style ends up blah and nothingy. This is bad for two reasons. Firstly, a strongly cut hairstyle gives you sharpness and looks very modern. Secondly, if a haircut doesn't have a strong shape and is just all one length, then it's very hard to do anything with it, unless you are an absolute whizz at hair styling. So, when you're running around having a manic day, you end up either scraping it back in a pony – which could be a waste of your crowning glory – or you spend hours faffing with it.

'Looking young, gorgeous and fresh is all about the detail of a haircut,' she continued. 'Talk to your hair-dresser – and other hairdressers – about a style that really suits your type of hair. A hairdresser should give you a consultation for free so you can go around and get the best advice to make a good decision before going for the chop. Ask for a really strong, well-cut hairstyle that just falls into place.'

A lot of people opt for bobs of various sorts. The fashions change every year and sometimes they will be chin length, which can be really flattering. Sometimes they will be shorter at the back or longer at the back, with a fringe or no fringe.

'Ask your hairdresser how you can give your style an update,' Pauline advised. 'You must tell them what you don't like. You can't just go in and just say, "I want a good haircut," because that doesn't really help them. You have to say things like, "I hate it when my hair is too short at the back, or drops over my eyes." Or, "I don't like it when it's a bit limp. I'd like it thicker on top." Taking along visual references can help.'

Somehow she persuaded me to have a fringe, even though I've got the tiniest forehead in the world and everybody said, 'You can't have a fringe. It will look like a little toothbrush!'

Her argument was, 'Your hair is so thick that if you don't have a fringe, you have no frame to your face and your tiny forehead is exaggerated, which doesn't flatter your face shape. It has to be cut in from a long way back from the hairline, which is a bit scary and a lot of hairdressers would be nervous about it, but I know your hair and know it will make you look so much better.'

And I think it does. So always make sure your hairdresser knows you well and knows how your hair naturally falls. Go to them a few times for a blowdry or trim before opting for any drastic change.

OK, now it was time to think about clothes. Over to my right, Debbie, our stylist and Head of Make-up and Wardrobe at *GMB*, was busy steam-ironing our gala outfits so they would be perfect for the red carpet. I called across to her for her words of wisdom on how to appear younger, which by now had become the main subject of discussion for everyone in the room.

'There are no rules to dressing young,' she said. 'You have to think about what flatters you. Don't buy an A-line skirt just because they are in. Go for pieces that fit really well, because they will make your shape look better.

'Clothes often look terrible on the hanger, so always try them on. Don't take a friend with you, because sometimes friends find it hard to be honest. They don't want to upset you and also they might think something looks nice even if it's not quite you. Although, having said that, you should be prepared to take little risks and see how they work.'

Debbie recommends looking at vogue.co.uk, which will give you a good sense of what is fashionable without having to shell out for the magazine. For instance, maybe tiger brooches are the latest thing and *Vogue* will feature one that is £500. 'Obviously, you won't buy that particular piece, but before you know it, Accessorize or Claire's Accessories will have something similar,' she said. 'Then you can team your dependably fab black dress with a tiger brooch that makes you look cool and current.'

'Fantastic, thank you,' I said.

'Now, let's talk about underwear, which is crucial,' she continued.

'Um, I think I'm sorted in that department,' I said, wincing slightly.

Perhaps unusually, it was a man who had given me the best advice in this area. My mind flashed back to a year or so previously when I was out on a shopping trip with my friend Nigel Boyd. 'If a woman wants to look good at any age, but particularly from midlife on, then they have to realise that it's all about what lies beneath,' he had declared.

I groaned. Not another man telling me that a woman's beauty comes from within! You know the sort of thing men spout when they're trying to get you into bed. 'It's the sparkle that makes a woman's eyes beautiful. It doesn't matter how many crow's feet you have. Anyway, I love your crow's feet.'

I have never really believed that. I've heard a lot of men's locker-room talk and I have never heard any of them say in private, 'Phwoar! You should see my girlfriend's crow's feet!'

'No, you fool!' Nigel said. 'I'm not talking about your soul, but something far more important – your underwear.'

We fell about laughing. Nigel is one of the few men who can talk about underwear without a hint of sex or smut. Perhaps this is because he's seen half of Hollywood and a big chunk of our British stars in their tighty-whities. After working in film and TV for a quarter of a century, nothing shocks him any more.

Nigel describes himself as 'an old rag picker from way back', which is industry slang for film and TV stylists and costumers. He has worked on films like *Forrest Gump, Saving Private Ryan, Ocean's Eleven* and *Iron Man*, and was mentioned by name at the Academy Awards when *The Artist* won a cluster of gongs, including the Oscar for Best Costume Design.

Nigel styles stars for the red carpet as well as for roles in movies, so I was keen to get his advice. 'It's obvious if you think about it,' he said. 'If you are dressing a star for a movie set in the 1920s, however much time and care you take with the outer costume, it won't look right if you put them in a bra and knickers from 2017. The cut and shape of the underwear pushes bits up or lets bits sag in a way that fits the fashion of the time.'

For instance, in the 1920s it was all about having a flat-chested boyish figure. So the bras didn't push you up and out; instead, many of them flattened you down. The pants flattened you too, with no attempt to cinch the waist. They were a break with the past, when couture had focused on tight corsets and tiny waists.

Another example is the Christian Dior post-war New Look, which was again all about the underwear. Breasts were hoicked up and out like pointy weapons using padded bras, and the petticoats had lots of netting at the bottom to make waists look even tinier.

'If you want to look good, younger and up to date, you have to get your underwear right,' Nigel said. 'And this goes double when the stars hit the red carpet. For big events, it's not unusual for the top designers to have mannequins made to the measurements of A-listers. Then they build the dresses from the inside out, designing the structure of their bras and undergarments before they fit the dresses over them. Of course, for a night like the Oscars, the stars make sure their bodies are in tip-top shape, but that alone isn't enough to make their frocks look great.'

I find it comforting that even the A-listers need help with getting their frocks to fall in the right way. At the 2002 Oscars, Kate Winslet wore a red strapless dress by Ben de Lisi and looked amazing in it. I interviewed her afterwards and, with typical modesty, she said it was all down to the dress because it had so much structure underneath. It was as much an achievement of architecture as dress design, she said, and the result was that it just flowed over her, as if it were effortlessly staying up.

This sadly wasn't the case with Gwyneth Paltrow when she attended the Oscars the same year. She was wearing a gorgeous Alexander McQueen gown, but the top was loose and she wasn't wearing a bra. Despite having an amazing body, the top half of her outfit had a rather sad droop and the papers were merciless the next day.

A lot of people swear by bras from Rigby and Peller, who boast that they supply underwear to the queen and the royal family. But they aren't cheap. You can get great stuff on the high street, but to look good on the outside I think you need real scaffolding on the inside – something that looks awful when you put it on, but has a transformative effect when you add clothes. I'm constantly on the hunt for a backless, strapless bra that holds you up in a way that doesn't bring to mind Barbara Windsor in *Carry on Camping*, but does give you that youthful mound, so you can wear a top with a bit of cleavage.

The closest I've been to having a dress designed and structured just for me was during my time on *Strictly Come Dancing*. When you sign up to the show, you get taken to a clothes house in South London, where they measure you with brutal honesty.

'I'm sure my waist isn't quite that big,' I ventured.

'Yes, it is,' said the assistant, 'and you will thank us for not fudging it. The last thing you want is seams ripping on the dance floor. You'll have enough to worry about.'

She was right about that.

Using my measurements, they built a multiway bra that was padded to the hilt and could adapt to backless, strapless, sideless and any other -less that the dresses might require. Each dress also had a stretchy, sparkly Spanx-type leotard sewn into it that kept everything in place as you were flipped upside down. I ended up skidding across the floor with my dress over my head during the samba and Len Goodman said it looked as though my partner, Anton du Beke, was mopping the floor with me. At that point, I didn't care about my score – I was just glad that my knickers were sewn in.

My all-purpose bra was a lifesaver and got me through several weeks of disastrous dancing. Why I kept getting voted back on to the show, I will never know, but I am so grateful because I loved it – and I was relieved that I managed to preserve my modesty through some awkwardly outrageous routines, if not my pride!

After that, I took my underwear a lot more seriously, although probably not as seriously as Nigel would have liked. 'People spend a fortune on dresses when they are going to big dos like their daughter's wedding. Then they'll put on the baggy old grey bra and knickers that they bought from a supermarket ten years ago,' he told me. 'If they are lucky, people will say, "Oh, what a beautiful dress, such a lovely colour!" Rather than, "Wow you look amazing!" Only the right underwear will get you that. You should look like you are wearing the dress, not that the dress is wearing you.'

I self-consciously fingered the strap of my supermarket bra. 'Will you help me with what lies beneath?' I whimpered.

The next thing I knew, we were in a department-store changing room and I was forcing myself into something that can only be described as a sausage skin. I started to sweat. I didn't like to mention that I had form with embarrassing moments in dressing rooms.

I flashed back to the time I hosted the *TV Quick* awards with Richard Arnold, about fifteen years ago, and the team at Debenhams in Oxford Street approached me and said they wanted to dress us. Richard and I were really excited about it.

In the Debenhams personal dressing department, Richard tried on a purple suit and looked great in it, so he was sorted. I then tried on a variety of purple and burgundy dresses to match his outfit. I found one that looked fantastic, but when I tried to take it off, the waistband got stuck on my breasts, which in those days were really perky and quite firm. I could not budge the dress over them.

I was sweating like mad and yelling, 'I can't get it off!' when Richard came in. All the Debenhams personal stylists were clustered round me, trying to help.

'We're just going to have to cut it off,' Richard said eventually.

'We can't!' they cried in chorus. 'It'll ruin the dress and it costs a fortune.'

In the end, poor Richard had to kneel at my feet, put his hands up the dress, hold my breasts down and squish them flat, while the store people pulled the dress over my head.

Thank goodness he's gay, I thought.

As for Richard, well, I suspect his thoughts were unprintable. 'This is *so* the last place I want to be right now!' he wailed. 'On my knees with my hands up your front, grabbing your breasts – I'm revolted.'

Since then I have never really enjoyed the process of going to personal stylists in stores. When they kindly offer to dress me for a function like the Baftas, I usually ask if they wouldn't mind sending a selection of clothes to my home so that I can try them on there in privacy.

Fifteen years after the Debenhams debacle, I found myself in a store with Nigel wearing a stretchy, flesh-coloured garment with shoulder straps, a high back and a low front that swooped under my bra, sheathed my tummy and hips and ended mid-thigh in a pair of sort-of cycling shorts.

I can't believe it has come to this, I thought.

When I was a teenager, I used to wear little lacy knickers. Then as a twenty-year-old, I loved G-strings. When I was pregnant and after I gave birth, I started to wear lovely cotton panties. OK, not as sexy as the lacy knickers, but still quite cool in a Calvin Klein-New York way. In the TV studio, I had always worn nude-coloured seam-free pants – not sexy, but at least they avoided any unflattering VPL (visible panty line) and they were below my tummy button. And now, suddenly, I was wearing knickers so big they went from my bra down to just above my knee. How had that happened?

'You'll love them,' Nigel said. 'They'll make all the difference in the world.'

I did. They were a revelation. I could buy a ten-quid dress from H&M in the flimsiest fabric and it would look much more expensive, a better cut and quality, because it glided over the lumps and bumps. They were a joy! After that, I was addicted. I wore my spandex body girdles all the time. I was hard-pressed to peel them off.

Best of all, as Nigel said, 'Nobody will ever know.'

Or so I thought.

In early March 2016, we were doing an item on *Good Morning Britain* that involved contestants jumping into an ice bath as part of a challenge called Tough Mums, a five-kilometre obstacle course run by celebrity mums, viewers and presenters. The presenter, Julia Bradbury, had a go and was brilliant, followed by our very own weather presenter, Laura Tobin, who was also brilliant.

As Susanna and Ben ended the show, we suddenly had an extra twenty seconds left after they said goodbye, because there's always a slight adjustment of timings before you hand over to the ad break. Just then, without any warning, Ben picked me up and swirled me round with the obvious intention of chucking me in the ice bath.

I started screaming my head off, largely because I had my phone in my coat pocket. I was thinking, 'Argh, if he throws me in, that's it – all my contact numbers, everything, gone!'

He obviously then thought better of it and swirled me back down to the ground. Susanna said, 'That's it, goodbye,' and everybody smiled at the camera.

As we finished, I looked up at the two floor managers, Dave and Sharon, who were staring at me with their eyes so wide they looked like they'd seen a ghost. 'Oh dear, that was terrible!' they said, shaking their heads.

'I know!' I laughed. 'I honestly thought he was going to chuck me in.'

'No, you don't understand,' they said. 'When he picked you up, we saw everything – and we mean everything. Even worse, when he put you back down, we saw everything again.'

'Everything?'

'Your crotch, your pants, everything.'

I was horrified. Suddenly my phone started pinging in my pocket as people tweeted pictures they had taken from their TV screens.

'I can't believe this, Ben,' I said, suddenly feeling very worried.

'Don't worry,' he said. 'I was holding you in a way that meant no one could possibly see anything.'

'Er... Look at this,' I said, showing him my phone.

He went white. 'Oh no, I'm so sorry.'

For the next hour, everybody at work kept saying, 'Oh no, oh no!'

Then the full horror dawned on me. The body girdle I was wearing was crotchless. Not for any dodgy or sexy reasons; it was just for practicality, otherwise how could you wee in it without getting completely undressed?

This was a lot worse than revealing big nude spandex pants to the world.

I then had to suffer the utter ignominy of sitting down with a producer to watch the whole thing back frame by frame and work out, as she put it, 'whether this was *Good Morning Beaver*, or not!'

I was teased for the rest of the day and it was even worse the following day, when people had had a chance to think up jokes overnight. I constantly had my head in my hands.

I have often been compared to Bridget Jones, because her dating disasters and calamitous moments seem to mirror my life. For the first Bridget Jones film, Renée Zellweger was sent tapes of *GMTV*, as it was then, with me presenting it, to analyse it for her role and prepare for the scenes where Bridget was working on *Big Up Britain*. Before she filmed the third movie, she came back and shadowed us again, and I spent time with her on set interviewing her in her fake Bridget Jones bedroom. When I arrived, she greeted me with, 'Ahh, the real Bridget Jones – welcome home! Do you like your bedroom?' It was alarmingly like my own, very messy and chaotic.

So there's been a long association with the Bridget Jones franchise and me, but it was especially exciting to have Renée laugh about it too. 'I think you have done everything that Bridget Jones has done, or maybe she has done everything you have done,' she said, 'apart from flash your knickers live on TV!'

Maybe she tempted fate!

Because now I had.

'I cannot believe it, Ben,' I said for the hundredth time.

'Look at it this way,' he said brightly. 'You've been moaning for ages that middle-aged women are invisible. At least now you've made everyone sit up and take notice!'

CHAPTER 5

The Art of Mastery

'Did you know that eight out of ten women say the thing they fear most about turning fifty is becoming invisible?' I said to my husband, as we sat down to dinner one date night.

'Who said that?' he said, quick as a flash. Ha ha, very funny.

At least I hope he was joking.

The weird thing about us midlifers fearing being invisible is that there are so darn many of us. Far from disappearing, we are literally in everyone's faces on every street corner.

In 2015, more than 20 million people in the UK were aged fifty years or over, out of a total population of 65. One million. That's roughly a third. Nearly eighteen per cent are over sixty-five; one million are over eighty-five. The fastest-growing group is people aged forty to forty-nine.

Perhaps part of the reason why we feel invisible is that no one seems to be proud of being middle-aged. It's not cool, it's not sexy – it's the subject of ridicule in many a bad sitcom and some good ones, too.

Hillary Clinton said of her husband's 1992 presidential campaign that of all the insulting press criticism she received during that period, 'the one that really hurt, and one of the few that was really true, is that I'm middle aged ... I couldn't believe I saw that in print.' She was forty-five.

If someone as intellectual and interested in far loftier issues than wrinkles (I imagine) as Hillary Clinton hates the term, what hope for the rest of us? Although I can't help thinking that after losing to Donald Trump twenty-four years later, in one of the most shocking election results in history, she might want to go back to that middle age – when she still had dreams of presidential power – and relish it.

Being middle aged isn't something our society aspires to. Everyone wants to be young. We are fascinated by youth – by its energy, its bouncy-skinned beauty, its bravery and its drive to leap higher, faster and better, without care. My daughter has always climbed too high up a tree for my nervous parenting, never fearing the branch will snap. And when one day it did, plunging her to the ground and shattering the bones in her left arm, she faced weeks of hospital treatment and surgery with amazing calm. While her dad and I lay awake at night feeling sick at what might have been, she loved getting her classmates to sign her cast. And although she cursed having to miss out on a term of being in the swimming team, she never questioned she would be back with a vengeance, always assuming she would be fine, that her bones would mend. Why would she doubt it?

Yet in midlife we know all about the consequences of things going wrong. We've had our hearts broken, likely our bones too. We may have had dreams shattered and realised we are not likely to be going to the moon; we may be wondering if in fact we ever really wanted to, because it suddenly looks rather uncomfy, that white rock, doesn't it? Not the glowing lure of mystery that it appeared through our childhood bedroom window.

Even if life is going well, we can't fully enjoy it, because flickering somewhere just out of our sight line, stuck in our blind spot like a cyclist at a left-hand turn, is the sense that at any time it could go wrong. Then comes that shock moment when fear brings it into focus, when you glance in the left wing mirror and are brought up short in a panic, thinking, 'What if I hadn't spotted that cyclist there? I could have killed him, or had a terrible accident!'

It's as if life is suddenly giving you the message: be careful, be cautious, it could all go wrong.

I'm not trying to depress anyone – I'm just exploring why we feel the way we do. It's not our fault. It's the images around us that lead us to feel this way. As I stared fifty hard in the face and came to the bleak realisation that I had fewer years left than I had already lived, it was hard to see the next few decades leading to anywhere particularly great. If midlife is midway, a kind of mid-point on life's journey, I can't help asking, midway to what? Old age? And, with it, all those negative associations of increasing ill health, loss of senses, loss of loved ones? I can't help shuddering at the thought.

We find ourselves asking, 'Is it all downhill from here?' And the answer seems to be a resounding yes. No wonder we want to run back through the door into youth. Skirt too short – who cares? Midlife crisis, affair with a younger man – so what? 'I am young, young, young!' it shouts. Or so we tell ourselves. But is anyone convinced? Are you?

The trouble is, by looking ahead and seeing only the negatives, we trap ourselves in a perpetual state of panic, trying to get our youth back. And largely that manifests itself as trying to 'look' young.

I see it all the time in my job. After the lively exchange of ageing tips that I'd instigated in the dressing room while we were getting ready for the ITV gala, we were finally primped and preened enough to face the cameras at the London Palladium. There was a long red carpet at the entrance this year, as there often is at awards ceremonies. On one side were the press and a bank of photographers, on the other were fans and autograph- and selfie-hunters. There was also a video camera, which filmed the procession of the stars as they walked down the red carpet and projected it on to a big screen outside, so that everyone could see and join in the glamour of the event.

The organisers wanted us to go down the red carpet in our programme groups. So the Loose Women were all together, the *X Factor* gang, the *Coronation Street* lot and the rest. While we were waiting for the *Good Morning Britain* group to assemble, we couldn't help looking at the big screen and commenting on the other stars.

'She looks great for her age, doesn't she?'

'Ooh, he's gone so grey!'

'Oh dear, she's had way too much surgery. She doesn't even look like herself any more. It's weird.'

'Wow, she looks amazing. What has she done?'

We were looking at our contemporaries and essentially 'marking' them on how well they were holding out against the passing of time; how effectively they were eradicating the natural changes like wrinkles and sags – how well they were managing their own decline.

But wouldn't it be wonderful if we didn't see any of these outward signs as 'decline' at all? If we saw old age as something to aspire to. If we associated it not with loneliness, decay, ill health and loss of usefulness, but with wisdom, learning, power and being at the centre of things? Then midlife wouldn't be seen as the beginning of the end, but as the start of a fantastic new chapter, as the springboard for a wonderful, fruitful and exciting part of our lives.

Of course in some societies it does have these associations. In many Native American communities, older members are revered for their wisdom and experience, and their advice is prized. All across India, elders are the heads of the family – and many Asian women leaders step into the limelight after menopause, when their knowledge and professionalism are even more highly valued. In these societies, older people are at the very centre of the community. Their advice is valued and their company sought, so the sense of isolation and loneliness isn't there, as it sadly is for so many over-seventies in our society. It's also interesting to note that in societies where older women are regarded as wiser and better, women report suffering fewer and less devastating menopausal symptoms, according to a study at Yale Medical School.

But we don't live in these societies – we live in good old Blighty, slap bang in the middle of the Western world. Such wonderful examples of old age and aspiration aren't so readily available. In fact, rather than being at the centre of our cultural lives, older people aren't even very visible, and nearly half of us think that older people are treated with more respect in other parts of the world.

When Betty Friedan wrote *The Feminine Mystique* in 1963, she opened up a whole new world of possibilities to women by challenging the way they were viewed as appendages to men. Now she has written an equally illuminating book on ageing, *The Fountain of Age*, and she argues that the way we view ageing now is even more deadly than the way we viewed women back in the 1960s. She conducted a study of prime-time network television in the US and monitored TV dramas for a week. Out of 464 character portrayals, only seven (1.5 per cent) looked to be sixty-five or older. In a similar vein, out of 290 faces in *Vogue* magazine, only one woman was clearly over sixty – and she was featured in a little inset entitled 'Me and Granny'. Out of 265 articles on ageing in a major Midwestern newspaper, none featured elderly people in a positive light; every article focused on problems.

Things aren't a lot better in Britain, either. A study conducted by the Creative Diversity Network for the BBC in 2012 found that female viewers over fifty-five were deeply concerned about the lack of representation of women their age and older on the television. Another study, two years later, found that only 15 per cent of the women featured on the most popular programmes on the main channels (including Sky 1) were over fifty-six, which in reality is half of the actual demographic. Men far outnumbered women and the women featured were more likely to be under forty than the men. What's more, older people generally are often represented as being technophobic (when in fact more than 50 per cent use Facebook) as well as being depicted as grumpy, forgetful, regressive and trapped in the past.

No wonder we stand at midlife and want to turn round and go back to youth. Added to the lack of positive role models in the media, we may also have some negative ones in our own lives – for example, parents and older loved ones, whose failing health is a source of sadness and responsibility. You may already have experienced loss, the grieving from which you haven't fully recovered. I am so lucky to still have both my parents in relative good health (touch wood, touch wood) but there isn't a day that goes by that I don't worry about what will happen to them and how I will care for them. I am plagued by the sense that time with them is running out.

So how do we midlifers shake off all this overwhelming negativity and get our 'heads right' to make the most of the rest of our lives?

Well, the first step, it seems to me, is to find our own 'elders'. That is, older role models who we can aspire to – who represent the sort of old age we would like to enjoy. And if our media and society won't light them up in neon, we have to look for them ourselves. We need them so that we don't spend our lives looking sideways at our contemporaries' sagging chins and comparing ourselves to them, or looking at those younger than us and feeling jealous.

Sometimes I think Keith Richards has the right approach to life: party hard; look like death (and not give a damn); and have a blood transfusion once a year. Although even he admits that 'Keith Richards' is something of a myth. Still, he has survived a lot of self-abuse with body and brain intact, and he's keeping fresh, still writing music, publishing a children's book, releasing solo albums and touring. Age isn't stopping him – that's the key.

'I always thought thirty was the end, until I turned thirty-one,' as he put it.

How can I be the nearest thing to Keith Richards that a 49-year-old mum of two can be, without taking off on the road with a punk band called the Midlifers and imploding within a week from drugs and lack of sleep?

I could look to Chrissie Hynde, perhaps. An iconic figure on the UK punk scene and founding member of The Pretenders, she brought out a solo album in 2014 that included contributions from Neil Young and John McEnroe. In the album cover photo she's got her hands on her hips, she's wearing jeans and warpaint, and she's saying 'Yeah?' with her eyes. I met her at an awards do and, after all these years, I still want to be her, just like I did when she was a poster on my wall as a teenager – and she's sixty-five.

Then there's Helen Mirren. Now she is a true 'elder', isn't she? When I first met her twenty years ago, I had just got my first job in national TV and was feeling excited but pretty wobbly, as if any minute someone would say, 'What are you doing here, interviewing an icon?' and send me packing, back to reporting on flower shows and school fêtes. She appeared to me back then to be a woman at her absolute peak, who had done and won it all. I remember saying, 'So, you've got all the awards then – Oscars, Baftas, Golden Globes and Emmys. Everything, in fact, apart from a Grammy. You haven't won a Grammy.'

'Not yet,' she said, with a twinkle in her eye.

You see, far from being at her peak, this was a woman still on her way up. There was no levelling off, no stagnating. She was then the age that I am now, and yet she seemed so much younger; ageless, even.

'The thing is,' said my friend Vickie White, who was producing that segment of the show that day, 'Helen Mirren is absolutely brilliant at what she does, and that transcends age. She is the master and it shines out. There's nothing needy about her. You don't feel she's desperate to be young – or desperate to be anything. She's just Helen Mirren.'

I've been lucky enough to meet her many times over the last two decades, most recently when she'd just turned seventy and become the face of a well-known skincare range. There she sat, on the *Good Morning Britain* sofa – gorgeous, glowing, utterly respected – and we asked her about how she felt about entering her eighth decade.

'Oh, for goodness sake,' she laughed, 'I don't even think about it. It's just a number.'

She still had the same twinkle but also, I thought, something extra – a new level of contentment. She talked about not rushing from one job to another, about relishing the gaps in between to refuel and have fun, and of taking time out to love her husband and cherish those close to her. There was no negative language; she didn't say she was too tired to work as much, or tired of the work, although it was clear that there was more to her life than being an actor. You felt she was utterly in control, but with a playfulness that you would more usually associate with a seventeen-year-old than a woman of seventy.

There is always the thrill of the unexpected in live breakfast TV interviews, but also the danger of guests unintentionally upsetting viewers because they forget what time of day it is and that children could be watching.

People don't want their kids to start asking awkward questions over the breakfast table. Helen Mirren's impish energy bounced off the studio walls as we rollercoastered through all sorts of subjects. A comment about a record period of wet weather sparked her to recall a wild affair she'd had with Liam Neeson, years ago, and how they'd camped in a tiny tent in the rain. At one point, she even swore (a big no-no at breakfast). My co-presenter Ben Shephard and I quickly apologised, fearing viewers would be offended. Her verbal slip did make the papers, but we needn't have worried – no one complained. Who could be offended? It was Dame Helen Mirren.

This playfulness made Helen fizz with youthful sexiness. OK, so maybe she wouldn't spark up a relationship with a twenty-year-old, although you suspect she could pull one – well, definitely a thirty-year-old anyway – but you also sensed she couldn't really be bothered. They would be judged wanting in her eyes, not the other way around. Her life was calmer these days, after having lived to the extremes of fun, of endeavour, indulgence and experimentation. And now she was reaping the rewards.

She looked utterly content, but still with drive, inquisitiveness and a feeling that the best was yet to come.

'That's the kind of woman I'd love to be at seventy,' I said to Ben, when the show came off air and we were wandering back to our dressing rooms.

'Dream on,' Ben said, flashing me one of his cheeky grins. 'Never mind seventy, I'd love you to be half that kind of woman right now.'

I have worked with Ben for the best part of twenty years and we love each other to bits, like brother and sister, and are fiercely protective of each other in the sometimes brutal world of TV. And, like a brother, he never misses a chance to tease or taunt me. Viewers love it and so do I – not least because I certainly give as good as I get!

But this time his words stopped me short.

He had a point. OK, so I was never going to be an Oscar-winning Hollywood star with the bank account to match, which probably helps Helen Mirren start her eighth decade more comfortably then most. But if I was going to be anything like the person I WANTED to be at seventy – content, satisfied, financially comfortable, healthy and seemingly complete in a happy relationship – shouldn't I feel on the road to that now? Instead, I felt far from it: overworked, constantly exhausted, worried I wasn't being the best at my job that I could be, or the best mum, stretched too thinly between home and work, and unable to remember when my husband and I last had a conversation about anything other than the 'business' of our family, let alone a good laugh.

Seeing my utterly crestfallen expression, Ben quickly said, 'Don't worry, there's only one Dame Helen Mirren.

She is the exception that proves the rule. You can't really expect to be like her; she is the master.'

There was that word again, 'master'. It was the same word my producer friend Vickie had used the first time I interviewed Dame Helen Mirren all those years ago.

But this time it seemed to me to mean more than just a comment about her acting. Ben was right: she was the master. The master of being, well, of being Helen Mirren; the very best version of herself, just as she wanted to be. That, it seemed to me, was true mastery. But how to achieve this extraordinary state of Yoda-like contentment, wisdom and age defiance? Especially as these days I felt like a master of nothing – never mind winning an Oscar, it felt like a triumph in my life if I left the house with my jumper on the right way and the kids wearing underwear.

'To claim your power, you have to confront the prejudices against ageing,' says my nurse friend, Anne. 'And I don't just mean society's prejudices, I mean your own, too. Science can help with this – giving you a better perspective. Medical advances mean that the old image of a stagnant, lonely, physically decrepit life beyond seventy is less likely to become reality.'

And this is not just about physical strength, but our mental capacity too. Marian Diamond, a Berkeley neuroscientist still researching in her seventies, has studied the effect of an enriched environment (lots of playthings and mazes) on the development of rats' brains. What you might call the 'enriched' rats – those who lived in the more exciting enclosures – grew larger brains, compared to the ones in standard wire cages. And 'enriched' older rats also showed big brain growth at a time when brain size normally diminishes. Diamond interprets her results as evidence that our brains maintain plasticity – the ability to make new connections – into old age.

Something's obviously got to get you in the end, as my granddad used to put it, but until then our lives can be ever fuller and richer, not smaller and sadder. 'There is no reason to think your next few decades will be ever more sedentary and marred by physical decay,' says Anne.

But you have to take action now.

'The first thing to realise is that it's you driving the bus,' said my friend Helen Warner, ITV's director of daytime TV, 'and I mean, *really* realise it. There is nothing wrong with standing in midlife and thinking it's downhill all the way. What's wrong with downhill? It's much better than an uphill struggle, I'd say! That is, of course, as long as you make sure you are in charge of the route.'

This made a lot of sense. It led me to reflect that society has a set of expectations for the first few decades of our lives, a pattern that we are all encouraged to follow. First, our parents tell us to brush our teeth and not wander into the road without looking. Then, teachers get us to stop daydreaming and pass some exams. Next, bosses make demands that we have to fulfil to the letter in order to get paid. Add into that the partners we want to win, or please. There are people above and around us, leading us forward. Even if you have never been a rule follower, this structure is present as a skeleton in our lives.

Suddenly we hit midlife and it disintegrates. We have either learnt all that these people have to teach us, or run out of ideas of how to please them. Our parents may well be the ones who need taking care of now, and even though we probably still have bosses they are likely to be ever younger and playing by a totally new set of rules.

This can be disconcerting, but also very liberating. That parent who meant to guide may also have intentionally, or unintentionally, controlled you. That teacher who insisted you did your homework may have got you through that maths test, but also forced you to give up a hobby you loved. Becoming a 'master' of yourself, it seems to me, is finding time to explore the things you didn't do, or left behind, and weave them back into your life, even if you feel your life is so crammed with responsibilities that there is no room.

Helen Warner has done exactly this with her writing. She is a hugely busy senior TV executive running a large team and overseeing more than eighty hours of TV a week. She is also a mum of two. Her commute from her home in Essex to the London TV studios meant she had an hour on the train both ways. She had previously filled the time with checking emails on the way in and fretting about family stuff. But she had also always wanted to be a writer. So she started writing stories on the commute instead. Now she has three best-selling novels to her name and arrives at work raring to go – because her creative juices are flowing from writing stories instead of dealing with the stresses of work problems in emails – and arrives home refreshed after a break from the pressure of her 'real' job.

Another TV producer, Ali Lutz, said that turning fifty was a revelation. 'All my life, I realise now, I had been trying to fit in, worried about saying the wrong thing in case I upset people or they thought I was stupid. Looking back, even the clothes I wore, often colours like black and grey, were about blending into the background. When I got to fifty, it struck me that I have never felt particularly rewarded for all that effort of fitting into a mould, certainly in terms of being promoted, so I just sort of gave up trying. I started wearing the clothes I liked and saying the things I wanted to say and people started noticing – in a good way. Before I knew it, it dawned on me that I was trusted and appreciated far more than I had ever realised. Suddenly I felt a whole new purpose and job satisfaction, and people actually said I looked younger too.'

But this new sense of liberation from rules also meant that I was beginning to realise that we can no longer blame those old 'authority figures' for the state of our lives, or use them as an excuse. If we are eating badly, never exercising and generally neglecting ourselves, then it's no use at fifty trying to give ourselves a let-out clause by saying, 'My mum overfed me,' or blaming an ex for saying we had chunky thighs, or whatever our demon is.

Tom Ford, the clothes-designer-turned-film-director, said recently, 'Most people over the age of fifty need a therapist, because the things you don't work out when you're younger come back to haunt you. You have to acknowledge them, realise them, forgive them and move on ... those things can consume you if you don't work them out.'

I'm not sure we all need therapy but his basic point is a good one. At fifty we have done an awful lot of living, loving and experiencing. That's a lot of stuff that will have affected us, and not all of it will be helpful. So it's time to embrace the things we want and let the other stuff go. As my friend Richard Arnold, the entertainment editor at *Good Morning Britain*, always says,

'You can't run a fresh, new bath if it's filled with old, dirty water.'

Time to pull the plug, heal old wounds, let go of regrets and embrace the new, I decided. But believing that age is an attitude, not a number, meant that if I was feeling old, it was my attitude that had to change. There was no getting away with it, I had to stop blaming time and Mother Nature and start being my own master.

I was daunted by the thought, but ready to give it a go. But first, I just needed to find the energy ...

CHAPTER 6

The Trouble with Sugar

It's not about how young you look, it's about how young you feel – so says absolutely everyone. My trouble was that I didn't feel young at all. I felt old and exhausted.

OK, my daily schedule was pretty tiring. I was getting up at a quarter past two in the morning to work on *Good Morning Britain*, presenting my daily live Smooth Radio show from ten to one, rushing to pick up the kids from school and only managing to get four or five hours' sleep a night at best. But was that any more draining than doing a twelve-hour night shift on a cancer ward? Or cooking for 200 people in a steaming restaurant kitchen, or ferrying obnoxious passengers around a city in a taxi? I don't think so.

So surely it couldn't be right to be feeling the way I was. Yes, I was turning fifty, but I honestly felt I had the energy of an eighty-year-old and life seemed to be spiralling out of control. One morning, I spent an hour in a total panic looking for the belt that I'd taken off the night before, only to find it in the fridge. Meanwhile there was a carton of milk on my chest of drawers.

This is not tiredness, I thought. I'm beginning to feel as if I'm losing my mind.

At work, a couple of days later, I was putting my head down for a five-minute desk snooze when my friend Clare Nasir, former *GMTV* weather presenter, now the face of Channel 5 weather, rang. 'How's it going? What's your forecast – cloudy with a chance of midlife blues?' she joked.

'Honestly? I feel at a physical low ebb,' I told her. 'I'm constantly exhausted. I feel like my children don't get enough of my time and I don't see my parents as much as I want to. I'm concerned that I'm not the best I could be at my job, because I'm frazzled. My skin's crêpey, my knees ache and I want a facelift.'

Hardly drawing breath, I continued pouring out my woes. 'A few weeks ago, I moved some boxes around, ripped a cartilage in my ribs and was instantly rushed to A&E and wired up to a heart monitor and a chest x-ray, because they looked at my age and thought it might be a heart attack. So that's where I am now. The thought of the next chapter of my life is just exhausting, with no light at the end of the tunnel ...'

There was silence down the phone.

'Are you still there?' I asked, wishing I'd just said I was fine.

'Actually, I'm just round the corner. Have you got time for a quick coffee?'

I grabbed my bag and hurried off for a fifteen-minute catch up between meetings. The next thing I knew I was sitting in a coffee shop staring at a new version of my old mate. I could hardly believe how fantastic Clare looked. She was totally transformed. Her cheeks were plumped up, her skin glowing and she had lost a dramatic amount of weight, yet looked healthy and beaming bright. What the heck?

'I've been on the keto diet,' she said with a grin. 'I feel amazing – I feel younger and fitter and my brain is more awake than it's ever been. The change has been so incredible that I'm writing a book about it.'

I got out my notepad.

'I'll email you my research,' she offered. 'You'll be fascinated.'

In some ways it's hard not to be a bit cynical when a friend tells you about their fantastic new diet, because there's a fresh eating fad in the press every day. It feels as if there has never been as much emphasis on eating well as there is right now, and every time I think we must be at peak You-Are-What-You-Eat, someone makes a new and inescapable link between diet, health and disease.

Some of the claims sound reasonable, others entirely ludicrous, and every December, the British Dietetic Association (BDA) duly puts out a list of the worst. The Super Elixir, the Sugar-Free, the Clay Cleanse and the Bulletproof diet all get the BDA thumbs down for being unscientific, vitamin-deficient or so difficult to stick to that they end up being socially isolating. Eat a spoonful of 'detoxifying clay' every morning? Start the day with a cup of coffee with a big lump of butter in it? It's pure whimsy, apparently.

But what do we really know about the effect that food has on our bodies? Once upon a time butter was good for you. Then butter was bad for your heart and everyone switched to margarine. Now we're back to butter again – so maybe we should start drinking it in our coffee? It's hard to know.

Twenty years ago we were advised to eat eggs in moderation because of their high cholesterol levels. Now it's gone the other way and we're told that eggs are a superfood, packed with vitamins, minerals, proteins and good fat. Basically, you can't eat enough of them – well, three a day is fine anyway (even if they're raw and you're pregnant, as long as they are British 'Red Lion' approved).

Fat used to be the enemy and carbohydrate a friend. Now they're swapping sides. It feels as if nutritional advice is constantly changing. Will we ever find out for sure what's really good for us?

The fat versus carbohydrate debate is interesting. The first time I started to think that eating too many carbs could be a problem was more than a decade ago, when a wave of books exploring the US obesity epidemic came out, including *Fat Land*, *Fast Food Nation* and *The Hungry Gene*, followed by UK writer William Leith's brilliant, agonising memoir about overeating, *The Hungry Years*.

It was quite a surprise back then to think that pasta and rice might not be good for you, but so often do I hear friends and colleagues say that they don't eat carbs these days that I barely register it. It's not news – it's Atkins, the Dukan, the Alkaline, the South Beach, the Gorilla ... OK, I made the last one up, but how long will it be before some clever nutritionist deduces that we should mimic the diet of our evolutionary predecessors and eat nothing but nuts, shoots and bananas? Not long, I'd guess, judging by the number of my mates who have been extolling the benefits of eating like a caveman on the 'Stone Age' Palaeolithic diet, which rules out all processed carbs and most other things apart from meat, fish and vegetables.

Wait, I've just checked online – you know, just in case – and found something called the Omni diet, based on the 70 per cent plant to 30 per cent protein ratio that gorillas eat in the wild. There are articles about the benefits of mimicking an apelike diet in the *Huffington*

Post and the *Daily Mail*. I am amazed. I literally made it up on the spot.

Perhaps I'd better do another sweep before I joke about the transformative powers of the plankton and krill diet, beloved of whale sharks, which works because we originally evolved from sea life. Where will it end? With the breatharians, who claim to have reached such a high level of consciousness that they get all their nutrients from the air? (They really do exist.)

I don't want to eat air! I want to eat food, and tasty food, at that. I must admit, though, that for a long time I have been haphazard, at best, with my diet. That wasn't always the case; I had a fantastic start in my childhood. We didn't eat fast food – to be fair, there wasn't a McDonald's or a Burger King anywhere near us in those days – and my mum would have never dreamt of buying ready-made meals. I am not sure they even existed in the way they do now. Also, my dad was a keen gardener and had an allotment, so he would bring home bundles of fresh home-grown vegetables, which meant not only did we get way more than our five a day, we also ate everything in season. As kids, my brother Matthew and I weren't keen on this. The runner bean season wasn't too bad, I loved those, but the purple sprouting broccoli and Brussels sprout seasons seemed to go on for EVER, despite my mum's best attempts at varying the menu. 'Sprout fritters, anyone?'

As a result of my parents' hard work, I was chock-a-block with good, healthy food throughout my childhood, which I am sure has given me a massive advantage health-wise. But it also meant, I am afraid, that I took a good diet and its positive effects totally for granted.

I remember one Christmas Eve, when I was about twelve, my probably totally frazzled mum said, 'You can have anything you want for tea, as long as it's quick and easy.'

In unison my brother and I piped up, 'Pot Noodle!'

I had never actually eaten one before, but we had seen the adverts. It looked cool, modern and rather magical, this meal in a pot that you made just with hot water. I think it broke my parents' hearts that, of all the wonderful food in the world we could have chosen from, we'd picked a dehydrated, chemically soaked kind of cardboard snack. But, true to her word, Mum let us have one, and I loved it. Wow, those overwhelming flavours and the fun of it coming in a pot!

When I went to college and took charge fully of what I ate, my taste for the 'naughty' could be really indulged. Last night's curry for breakfast, perfect! Pizza for lunch, burger for dinner and a kebab on the way home from the pub – hooray. No one was there to suggest a broccoli or a carrot should be thrown in as well and I made the most of it. Add into that my fun, exciting nightly visits to the student union bar and, as you can imagine, my weight ballooned. I had started freshers' week at just over eight stone, which was probably about right for my five foot two petite frame. I came home for the summer holidays at way over eleven, feeling horribly sluggish and unhealthy.

I remember my mum's face when I walked through the door with the obligatory huge bag of dirty washing. 'You look different. Have you done something to your hair?' she ventured, not quite wanting to state the obvious. But we both knew.

A summer of Mum's cooking and loads of exercise got things back on track, but gaining weight had shaken me up and changed my relationship with food forever. I was now horribly conscious of how easy it was to go way over 'curvy' and how hard to get my old slim self back. I started analysing the food I ate rather than just enjoying it – measuring a 'good eating day' as one where I had 'resisted' all the naughty food I loved, in the process making it seem even more desirable, like delicious forbidden fruit. I didn't quite go to Bridget Jones's extremes – one day 15 calories and another 8,450 – but there was quite a bit of unhealthy yo-yoing.

Pregnancy helped – you have to make peace with massive weight gain then and you want to eat well to do your best for the tiny life inside you. Then, of course, as I weaned my babies on to solids, the last thing I was going to give my tiny miracles was anything other than the purest, healthiest food. But as for myself, I still didn't really take on board the healthy message. I felt so bombarded with dietary advice – advice that always seemed to make me feel guilty about the 'naughty' food I secretly preferred – that I just sort of switched off and stopped listening. I ate what I fancied, made sure I didn't eat too much of it and put all my attention into making sure the kids ate well. Half the time, I ended up just clearing up what was left on their plates, because it was easy.

But now, with my energy and health at a new low ebb, even I could see this really wasn't good enough any more. I couldn't put my head in the sand any longer. I had just woken up to the idea that in order to live and love the rest of my life, I had to be 'master' of myself – and that meant taking control of my diet, too.

And so with Clare sitting in front of me looking amazing and totally transformed, I forced myself to listen. 'The ketogenic – or keto – diet is all about good food, and especially good fat,' she told me.

She went on to explain that it's a high fat, medium protein, low carbohydrate programme invented in the 1920s by Dr Henry Rawle Geyelin, one of the first doctors in New York to combat diabetes with insulin. The diet was originally developed to help in the treatment of epilepsy, with a lot of success. It was also found to be good for weight loss, reducing inflammation and boosting cell efficiency. Now it's the subject of intense research in Sweden and other countries because studies are showing that it may be able to help or even reverse Alzheimer's, memory loss and cancer.

Pretty mind-blowing claims, then.

Some scientists believe that the surge in Alzheimer's diagnoses is due to the overuse of sugar in the last twenty or thirty years, when everybody went crazy about low fat and our foods filled up with salt, sugar, and refined and complex carbs. (For this reason, they sometimes refer to Alzheimer's as type 3 diabetes.) Fat went out of favour just after World War II, when research began to link foods containing saturated fats to heart disease. Eggs and red meat were out; vegetables, fruits, beans and whole grains were in. But that meant carbohydrates were in too and, by extension, refined carbs like white bread and white rice, which was where the obesity problem started, some claim.

The keto diet works by replacing carbs with fat, which lowers blood sugar and insulin levels and encourages your body to burn fat instead of glucose for energy. Crucially, the body also turns fat into ketones in the liver, and ketones have been shown in studies to stop the brain degenerating.

I LOVE the idea of a diet that can protect against Alzheimer's and senile dementia, because that's very high up on the list of everyone's fears about old age.

And whatever your age, Clare says, the keto diet boosts brain power, collagen and elastin. That might well translate into no more putting belts in the fridge, and Clare says that her wobbly bits have gone too. She says she has been losing bad fat and putting on good fat – and her skin feels younger and tighter.

How soon can I start?

But wait. Is there a downside? Going on the ketogenic diet in its strictest form requires medical supervision, especially if you have an existing health condition like diabetes. It can be a shock to the system to cut out sugar and carbohydrates altogether and some people could experience an extreme reaction. There's also a certain amount of fasting involved, as there is on the 5:2 and so many other diets. All the current trendy diets seem to be about starvation, because it can be very healing to give your body a break from the complex business of digesting food.

The Ancient Greeks were big fans of fasting. Hippocrates, Aristotle and Plato all practised it. Intermittent fasting has now been proven to enhance growth and fat-burning hormone secretion, which encourages weight loss and muscle gain. There is evidence to show that it stimulates your metabolism, lowers blood sugar levels to protect against type 2 diabetes, and reduces inflammatory markers and LDL cholesterol (bad cholesterol) thus helping to prevent heart attacks and stroke.

It also promotes cellular repair. Much of the research is still in its early stages, but fasting may also be a useful tool for warding off cancer and Alzheimer's – and it seems to extend the lives of rats and monkeys, so the chances are that it would work on a couple of my ex-boyfriends. It's not recommended if you're under-weight, have eating issues or are trying for a baby, though. And if one of your mates gently takes you aside and tells you that you're overdoing it, listen.

The most popular way to fast intermittently is the 5:2 diet, where you eat normally for five days of the week, but on the other two (non-consecutive) days you only allow yourself 500–600 calories. It definitely works for some, whether you're the TV chef, Hugh Fearnley-Whittingstall, who embraced it a few years ago and slimmed down dramatically, or my mate Joe's mum, Elaine, who lost two stone in five months and has never looked back. I think it's effective because you soon realise that you don't need a huge amount of food to keep you going on your 'fasting' days – and maybe your stomach shrinks, or you learn restraint, or maybe it's the fact that you simply pause and think about what you're putting into your body that then transforms your approach to eating.

Other popular fasting programmes include the 16/8 method, where you only eat during an eight-hour period – say, 12–8 p.m. – and fast for the other sixteen hours. The downside of this is that you skip breakfast, which we're told is the most important meal of the day. Although that's nothing compared to the Eat-Stop-Eat diet, where you fast for twenty-four hours twice a week, skipping breakfast, lunch and dinner. After that, we're in breatharian territory once more.

It's definitely becoming clear to me that at this age dieting is less about trying to shrink yourself into skinny jeans and more about eating for health. But there are lots of diets out there that make health claims and, frankly, it's very difficult to know which one is best, because we are all individuals. I guess you need to identify your weak spots, think about your family history of illness and research the claims and their authors before you decide which one is right for you.

The Mindspan diet sounds interesting. It's been devised by Dr Preston W. Estep who, as director of gerontology at Harvard Medical School's Personal Genome Project, has pretty unassailable credentials. Looking for ways to ward off mental decline and forgetfulness in old age, Estep studied diet and culture across the world and found that Japan had the best record for sharp cognitive functioning in later life. As a result, he advocates all the usual 'good' foods, like green leafy vegetables, beans, pulses and reduced sugar intake, but also *white* rice, pasta and bread, and fermented foods like vinegar and pickles, which the

Japanese love. Another key element of the Mindspan diet is to avoid foods that are high in iron, even if they have other healthy benefits. He thinks that most adults in the developed world have too much iron in their diet, which is OK for women up until menopause, because menstruation keeps iron levels down, but could have dire consequences for brain health later on.

Estep's theory is beguiling – and we all know the Japanese have a great diet. But there's also been a lot written about the benefits of the Mediterranean diet, which feels closer to home and perhaps more enticing. My friend, the author, nutritionist and food presenter, Tonia Buxton, is a huge advocate – and she knows a thing or two about healthy eating. In 2014, when she was forty-six, she was told by a Harley Street specialist that she had the fertility levels of a woman in her early thirties. 'The doctor said I had enough eggs to keep giving birth naturally into my fifties,' she laughs. She is convinced – and so was her doctor – that her diet was a contributory factor.

This makes me feel slightly jealous, actually. I can't help wishing that I hadn't left it until now to take more interest in what I eat, for the sake of my health and internal workings, rather than slimness. If I had, would I have been able to have that third baby I'd craved?

'Who knows,' says Tonia, 'but this is not about anyone else, not even another baby – this is about you doing the best for you. Don't ever think it's too late to sort your diet out. Whatever your age, if you make the changes right now, you can transform your health for the rest of your life. Of course, you may well regret that you didn't do it earlier, but it's better to start now than in five years' time.'

A mum of four, Tonia looks staggeringly young for her age and puts it down to a diet rich in food that contains anti-inflammatories and antioxidants, like olive oil, garlic and turmeric. 'As you get older, your body gets more and more inflammation, which prevents you from feeling youthful,' she says. 'Aches and pains are caused by inflammation and cell damage, while the skin can also get inflamed. Preventing the oxidisation of your body helps reduce this – and the less inflammation and cell damage you have, the younger you look and feel. Most children have next to no inflammation.'

Meanwhile, Tonia's kitchen is redolent with delicious aromas of meatballs and stuffed peppers, broccoli, spinach, pine nuts and cheese. This is a woman who would never dream of eating an ordinary chocolate bar snack, but still drinks a glass of red wine every evening. 'Lifestyle is as important as diet,' she tells me. 'When I was in my twenties I was really into fitness. Now it is all about living a holistic life.'

It's interesting that she mentions the well-known anti-inflammatory properties of turmeric. Herbs have been used medicinally across the world for millennia, in Traditional Chinese Medicine, the Ayurvedic system, South America, Africa and old English apothecaries. Most people know that ginger is good for the stomach and throat, garlic for warding off colds and stinging nettles for rashes and joint pain – but it's less widely known that coriander combats bad cholesterol and bay leaves are good for sinus infections. The list goes on, so I've treated myself to *The Complete Book of Herbs*. Once I've memorised it, I'm tempted to change into flowing robes, grow a couple of warts on my nose and sit cackling over a steaming cauldron. Watch this space.

Returning to diets, I decided to try the keto diet because Clare looked so fantastic, and she seemed very confident that it would improve my mental acuity and tiredness. I also wanted glowing skin. I didn't think I needed to lose much weight, but shedding a few pounds wouldn't go amiss and I liked the idea of zapping the bad fat caking my thighs and tummy by eating good fat. Any woman in her forties will know what I mean by that.

First, I have a question. What is the difference between good fat and bad fat? It used to be stated as fact that the good fats were monounsaturated and polyunsaturated, and the bad fats saturated. But butter, a saturated fat, is now regarded as a good fat, so things have become a little confusing. Good fats can be found in avocados, eggs, nuts, olive oil, cream, coconut oil and oily fish. Bad fat is often fried fat and gets stored as globs in the very places you don't want it. It is also advisable to avoid trans fats and anything that is partially hydrogenated. Like the devil.

OK, I'm ready to begin.

Clare advised me not to go too crazy to start with. She suggested eating lots of high fat foods and a moderate amount of protein, like lean meat and fish. There was to be no sugar or fruit – and that meant no milk in tea or coffee, because milk contains sugar – no pasta, rice, couscous or starchy vegetables like carrots or potatoes, and no alcohol. For someone who often makes do with the kids' leftover pasta, it was going to be quite a challenge.

Years ago a chef told me that organic butter is the best thing to cook with, because it remains stable at incredibly high temperatures. Since I've often been told that olive oil denatures when it's hot – it doesn't do anything bad to you, but it loses all its good properties – I decided to give cooking everything with butter a crack.

Here's what happened:

DAY ONE

My first big shock was that everybody at *Good Morning Britain* thinks I'm a total sugar fiend.

'You'll never be able to give up sugar! You're completely addicted to it,' they laughed.

'I'm not. I don't really eat sugar,' I said in surprise.

Eyebrows went up all around the studios. 'You're a total chocolate monster!' Ben said.

'Not true!' I protested.

'Come on, you've got a titanic sweet tooth,' one of the sound guys chipped in. 'It's bigger than a woolly mammoth's tusk.'

This was really perplexing. 'What rubbish! I don't even have sugar in my tea.'

Susanna gave me a sceptical look. 'Have you forgotten that Darren, our fabulous cameraman on camera two, brings you a pile of crew chocolates every morning before you go on-air?' she asked.

'Yes, but ...'

Does that count? I've worked with Darren Bramley on *GMTV* and other programmes for twenty years and I've always thought it was a loving gesture to bring me chocolates in the morning. Everyone likes a bit of chocolate, don't they? If you get up early and you're knackered, or you work shifts, or your baby has cried all night, then a little bit of sugar works wonders, doesn't it?

Admittedly, I hadn't really noticed that I was in the habit of reading the news with my Celebrations tucked behind me, handily placed so that I could snaffle them one by one during the ad break. 'But it doesn't make me an addict, does it?' I argued.

Cue mass hilarity among the crew. 'Is the Pope Catholic?' my producer quipped, tears of laughter streaming down her face. 'Do one-legged ducks swim in circles?'

I genuinely couldn't understand what was causing all the merriment. I thought hard for a minute. OK, sometimes, pre-children, I used to go out late partying, get up early, do the breakfast show, come home and sleep – and when I woke up from my day nap, I would be so exhausted that I'd literally eat Tate & Lyle sugar cubes out of a bowl to revive me. It was like coming up from the bottom of an ocean of tiredness and confusion and the sugar was my oxygen. One or two cubes later, I'd come to, feel great again and begin the process of preparing for work the following day.

But that was then.

'And these days you eat chocolates for breakfast!' Ben said.

Was he saying that sugar has been entirely part of my life and I haven't even noticed it? That my sugar levels have been going up and down all day for many years? We've done two strands on *Good Morning Britain* about cutting out sugar and I've resolutely refused to take part in both of them. I didn't feel I'd be a good guinea pig as I wasn't overweight and was convinced that I ate a reasonably balanced diet. But it turns out that I've been fuelling myself with pure Tate & Lyle.

For the rest of the morning, members of the crew were walking past me sniggering and saying things like 'Is the sky blue?' and 'Have you heard about what bears do in the woods?'

Gosh. I've genuinely never thought of myself as addicted to sugar, but it appears I am. I'm starting to realise that all this time I've been managing tiredness by short-term energy bursts from sugar.

'OK, I confess,' I said finally, throwing up my arms in surrender. 'My name is Kate and I'm a sugar addict.'

A cheer went up around the studio.

My friends say they've never seen me eat a proper meal in their lives, which isn't quite true – it's just that my natural meal times don't match everyone else's. I've never been a breakfast, lunch and dinner person because I'm always somewhere weird when it's everyone else's breakfast, lunch and dinner. So I've never had that proper sit-down routine for meals, and actually if I do eat lunch I always feel a bit sleepy, get cross with myself and think, 'I can't do anything now, I'm really tired.'

It's dawning on me that I eat sugar when I'm slumping so that I can carry on, but I don't eat a whole meal because that will make me sleepy – unless I'm either going for a nap or going to bed, when I'll eat enough to knock me out. I am realising that I have been using food to manage lack of sleep by injecting sugar into my body – almost self-medicating – to give myself a boost when I need to wake up. I then fill myself up so that I go all drowsy when I need to get to sleep. It's time to stop.

It's probably not helping my mood either. Today I read that 90 per cent of serotonin – the 'feel-good' hormone – is produced in the digestive tract. Sorry about the pun, but it's definitely food for thought.

DAY THREE

I've discovered that eating a sugar-free breakfast is very tricky when you're busy. And even harder if it's at a time when most people are asleep. What is handy? I used to swipe some of the food from the green room at *GMB*, which was really for the guests. Quick fixes like croissants, buns, cereal and toast – but these are now all out, because they're full of sugar and carbohydrates. I tried bringing in a boiled egg, but it's fiddly to remember to boil it the night before and also to remember to get it out of the fridge at 2.30 in the morning. Plus they stink.

Ben was disgusted. 'What fresh hell is this new breakfast?' he asked, wrinkling his nose as I peeled the shell off my egg at 3.30 a.m. I should add that he has already (pre-diet) banned me from eating toast and Marmite, because he hates the smell of Marmite first thing, too.

I pointed out that it could be worse. Clare had recommended oily fish like mackerel or pilchards and advised me to carry a tin of fish around in my bag in case a sugar-free food option wasn't to hand. This shut him up for a while, but didn't stop him ostentatiously spraying room fragrance around the newsroom.

DAY FOUR

This morning I brought in an avocado, which has good fat, omega-3, potassium, riboflavin and Vitamins A, B, C and E among its dizzying array of nutrients. It's the Chitty Chitty Bang Bang of fruits – a single-seeded berry, to be exact – and it's filling and quick to eat. But avocados are fraught with trauma. You buy them and they're too hard. Then they're suddenly ripe and get squished in your handbag. So far I've ruined two forms that I was supposed to fill in for Darcey to take back to school – now smeared with avocado mush – and a beautiful purse that Derek bought for me. The whole thing is rife with annoyance.

'We can get you scrambled eggs from the canteen,' the floor manager Simon White said, 'if you hold on till half seven when it opens.'

It was pretty damn nice of him to offer. Great, I thought, they'll be easy to eat in the ad breaks or during reports.

Not as easy as I'd imagined, though, because Ben made me stand in a corner of the studio with my plate. 'It is not unreasonable to eat scrambled eggs in the morning,' I protested.

'It is!' he said, looking outraged. 'Nobody wants to smell that, and the guests might think it's you that smells, or even worse, me!' His expression softened to a sympathetic smile. 'I am proud of you for trying – just keep a minimum of two metres away from me!'

By the end of the day, my stomach felt hard and inflated. It was really disappointing, because it was the opposite of what I wanted. I figured it was probably because I wasn't eating any fruit. And do eggs block you up?

DAY TEN

I went into my local health food shop yesterday and saw ketones supplements! They're being sold as a weight-loss aid, but haven't been clinically tested on humans (only rats) and there's no proof that they actually work. Meanwhile, I've noticed that I'm losing weight, but it could just be simply because I'm eating less rubbish – no cakes, chocolate or crisps. There are no snacks that work on this diet because they all have something forbidden in them, which means you end up eating a much purer selection of food. I'm not sure yet whether it's the introduction of good fats that's the positive of the keto diet, or just the fact that if you don't eat sugar or carbohydrates you naturally eliminate all the bad stuff.

I'm feeling full even though I'm not eating huge amounts, which must be the advantage of eating fats. I've got avocados coming out of my ears, frankly. Which is great for me but perhaps not so good for the planet, because they require a lot of water to grow. We're consuming nearly 50 million avocados a year in the UK. Avocado sales are overtaking orange sales. They're a staple of the so-called hipster diet, which requires you to have avocado mash on toast at least once a day. They are wildly popular on Pinterest and Instagram, a favourite of Gwyneth and Nigella, and there's even a pop-up restaurant in Clerkenwell, London, where you can eat five avocado courses in one meal, including avocado soup, ice cream and cocktails. It's all about the good fat. People are calling it a fetish. It's weird. I feel as if I'm becoming obsessed with them.

It's funny, because I remember being warned off avocados twenty years ago, when everyone started saying, 'Don't be fooled! They're full of fat!' People didn't understand about good fat then. All the really attractive food was low cal; diets were about calorie counting.

I started out eating my avocados with balsamic vinegar until I realised that it has a lot of sugar in it. They're fine to eat on their own, though. I'm also eating a lot more meat than I usually do. I've been trying to stick to chicken, but I cooked a beef casserole for Derek and the kids at the weekend, picked out the meat and ate it with salad.

At some point I should do the starvation part of the diet, when I'm not supposed to eat for five days. Not sure how I'll manage it, what with everything else I have to do. I've always been somebody who eats little and often – grazing, I try to convince myself pompously, but really it's just snacking. I think that's partly because of the weird hours I work and my habit of propping myself up with sugar. It's a problem if you're forcing your body not to work at its natural rhythm, which we all are, fundamentally. We're all trying to fit into society's day rather than the timetable that suits us individually. So when your body slumps in energy and seems to signal, 'Eat something, please!' you probably just need to go to bed. But of course that's not possible if you happen to be at work, so you grab a KitKat instead.

While I've been on this diet, I've purposely not eaten anything just before going to bed and I've gone to sleep OK – I haven't been struggling to drop off. And you know what? My energy is coming back and I'm feeling calmer.

DAY TWELVE

I had a banana yesterday, even though I'm not supposed to eat fruit. It was early in the morning and there was nothing around that fitted my diet and I thought, I've got to eat something or I'll start to feel sick.

What surprised me was how incredibly sweet it tasted. I'd never thought of bananas as particularly sweet before, which shows how quickly my palate has changed. It reminded me of a mortifying moment I had on-air, while we were doing a sugar-free story on *Good Morning Britain*. I had refused to go sugar-free. 'It's ridiculous. What's wrong with a bit of something sweet now and then?' I argued, partly because I felt I should speak up for the many people watching who would be thinking the same thing as me. But Susanna was doing it religiously. God love her – on message, on board.

Susanna brought some sugar-free cakes into our morning meeting and offered me one.

I wasn't impressed. 'Disgusting! It's literally like eating cardboard,' I said.

'It tastes delicious to me,' Susanna said happily. 'I think I've retrained my palate.'

We went on-air, started chatting about the sugar-free diet and checked in with our family who were trying to lose weight. Tonia Buxton, the nutritionist on the item, was with them in their home, so we linked up to the studio via satellite and Susanna said, 'Now, I had a cake this morning that Kate also tried—'

'Yes,' I interrupted, 'and it was absolutely rank. I don't know how you could eat it, Susanna! I don't get this sugar-free stuff.' Unbeknownst to me, Tanya had actually made the sugar-free cakes herself...

'I made that cake,' Tonia said, looking like I'd shot her pet. If ever there was a moment when I wished the ground could swallow me up! I started apologising profusely live on-air.

'Susanna thought it was delicious, though!' I said, desperately trying to dig myself out of my hole.

Now that I have retrained my palate too I've begged Tonia to make another batch for me to try. 'I was poisoning my palate with the crew chocolate!' I said in my defence. 'Your cakes will taste utterly delicious to me now, I know it.'

DAY FIFTEEN

I've stayed away from alcohol for two weeks so far. But today I was going to a friend's birthday and wasn't sure I could stick to it. Derek offered to get me a glass of wine from the bar.

I felt a bit depressed as I said, 'I'm not allowed to have wine.' I didn't want to be THAT person, the one who can't even have fun because they are so conscious about their diet. The words sounded rigid and unbending.

Then I remembered Clare saying, 'You can have gin because it's low in sugar, as long as you drink it with fizzy water.'

So I had a gin fizz, without the lemon, and felt better.

The truth is, I don't really drink that much these days. I mean, I still love to get 'seriously squiggly' as my mum used to say, on a big night out with my mates, but a while ago I realised that I can't drink the night before I get up early any more. I used to be spectacularly good at it before I had children. I'd party till one, have an hour's kip, go into work at two and be OK. The only side effect was swollen ankles, as I remember – it was always quite hard to get my shoes on. I never had a problem going out for lunch the next day and starting all over again.

About three years into my time at *GMTV*, the presenter Penny Smith warned me that I was heading for trouble. 'You can drink at lunchtime or you can go out late at night, but you can't do both. You'll either slip up on-air or make yourself really ill.'

'OK,' I said. 'Good point.' And I stopped.

I've never been a single glass of wine every evening person. It just makes me feel sleepy. My view has always been, I want to drink alcohol to party or I might as well not bother. I'm a social drinker. I don't do it to change my mood.

These days, I go out late very rarely, and my big lunches with the girls are organised around childcare responsibilities. 'Are you picking the kids up from school, Derek? Yes? Great, I can let go and have a drink.'

DAY TWENTY-ONE

This is my last day on the keto and I'm certain it's done me good. I've been eating less, drastically reduced my sugar intake and cut out all the other rubbish in my diet. I don't miss the sugar because I feel loads better – I'm a lot less 'slumpy', so I'm not constantly craving something sweet to give me a boost. I've found that the protein in eggs and fats offers longer-term energy. I've felt fine having avocado when I get in for work at about 4 a.m. and then eggs at 7.30 a.m. while we're on-air. I haven't hit my usual ten o'clock slump. It feels good to be making conscious choices about what I eat.

But the diet is too extreme for me because I think there's nothing wrong with good sugars – with eating an apple or a banana, say – and I want to have a tomato or a potato occasionally. I also understand that it's not ideal to eat an entire packet of chocolate digestives or a bumper bar of Cadbury's Dairy Milk, as I secretly used to love to do – and not just because you'll get a bit chubby, but because you're not giving your body any tools. When you're young, you can overcome everything with your cells' brilliant youthful regenerative energy, but when you're older, you can't.

Fundamentally, these three weeks have been about eating less and eating good stuff. So if I were asked to write an anti-obesity diet campaign, I would headline it: EAT LESS and EAT GOOD. I don't want to encourage under-eating (and I didn't try the starvation part of the diet because it had to be done under medical supervision) but I think we have to face up to the fact that most people overeat in the Western world. Essentially, you're going to feel better, get rid of the bits of you that wobble that you're not keen on and stabilise your risk of developing type 2 diabetes if you EAT LESS and EAT GOOD. Anything else is a trick.

If it suits you to organise that by having five days of eating what you want and two of having a very restricted intake, brilliant. If you decide to follow the Mediterranean diet, because nothing could be more delicious to you than organic olives and goat's cheese, fantastic. If you want to do the ketogenic diet, because you feel like you need to get your body under control, like I felt I needed to, that's great too. But make sure you eat as much of the good stuff as you can. Don't be afraid of fats but make them good ones and your skin is bound to benefit.

There has been a lot of scrutiny of the places in the world where people live to be over a hundred and stay healthy and relatively cancer-free. Places like Ikaria in Greece, Okinawa in Japan and Loma Linda in California, where the inhabitants have very distinct cultures and diets, but share certain crucial elements. A sense of community seems to play a massive part. Family and religion are also central, as are taking time to de-stress and have fun. As for diet, it's all about eating the good stuff, and not too much of it. That's how I intend to eat from now on.

CHAPTER 7

'Get Off That Sofa, Garraway!'

'What next, now you've sorted out your diet?' asked my super-fit, super-healthy friend Clare Holt as she sipped her extra-skinny de-caf soy latte through a straw. 'Don't tell me you've joined a gym,' she said, wincing slightly.

'I have,' I beamed. 'It's the logical next step. I'm determined to get fit.'

'I'm not sure I like this new you,' she said. 'You're Kate: the clumsy, calamitous one, who will always choose a slice of chocolate cake and a comfy sofa over anything physical. It's just not right.'

Then she perked up. 'Mind you, have you actually been yet?'

'Goodness, is that the time?' I said, hurriedly looking at my watch. 'I'd better get back to work.'

It's a bit of a joke among my friends that, although I'm very busy, active and constantly rushing around all over the place, I've always struggled to fit any 'real' exercise into my life. As a kid, I wasn't naturally sporty – I was the sort who would flinch rather than run towards the hockey ball and was the last to be picked for any team. As an adult, I have tried though ... Well, sort of. Every New Year's Day, I wake up full of motivation and write a list of get-fit resolutions. Last year, I even laminated them and stuck them on the fridge. Unfortunately, they were still there in March, yellowing and peeling, with every resolution broken. I meant to keep them, but then daily life would kick in and something else would be so much more urgent and important to do at that moment.

I guess that could be everybody's excuse, couldn't it? And not a very original or modern one, either. More than a hundred years ago, the politician, Edward Stanley, observed that people weren't looking after themselves, and said, 'Those who think they have no time for bodily exercise will sooner or later have to find time for illness.' Ouch.

Clearly, I needed further convincing to change my ways and make exercise a part of my life. So I did my research and, yep, there's no escaping it. Exercise is good for you in so many ways that the benefits are impossible to ignore, especially as you get older. You've got to keep moving, otherwise you're lining yourself up for one of those big deaths that we all dread. You know, heart attack, cancer, stroke – the ones that you shudder even to think about. Avoiding a big death means of course trying as much as possible not to smoke or drink too much, not to put on too much weight or overdo it in the sun. It's important to have regular check-ups, too. But exercise tops every expert's list of what you need to do in order to stay healthy and fabulous for as long as you can.

Are you ready for this? There is hard evidence that getting fit dramatically lowers the risk of heart disease, diabetes and cancer. It keeps the weight off, relieves tension and improves energy levels. It gives you a sharper memory and boosts levels of the chemical messengers dopamine and serotonin, which not only make you feel good but also help your brain cells communicate with each other. It stimulates chemicals in the brain that help new cells to grow and reduce harmful changes caused by stress. In terms of health, it's the gift that keeps on giving, all your Christmases come at once.

Why is exercise so crucial? Why isn't resting just as effective a way of preserving our bodies' strength, energy and essence? Nobody knows for sure, but one theory is that we were originally nomadic and so we're hardwired to keep moving in search of food, water and shelter. Heartbeat, blood flow, cell health and happiness all seem to have a link with regular, moderate exercise, so perhaps our bodies think that unless we're moving, we've given up in some way – that we've decided to stop foraging and lie down and die instead.

When you put it that way, exercise becomes as life-affirming as sex or laughter. And like sex and laughter, it gives you a glow. Regular aerobic activity can actually transform the protein structure of your skin, according to researchers at McMaster University in Hamilton, Ontario. This is great news as you get older, when your skin barrier function gets weaker and your cells need more help with staying hydrated. A good moisturiser is essential, but the researchers at McMaster University found that jogging or cycling twice a week helps the skin texture of fifty- and sixty-year-olds more closely resemble that of people aged twenty to forty, whose cellular senescence (old age) hasn't kicked in yet. How completely fantastic. Where's my bicycle pump?

It's not just your complexion, it's everything. Ben Shephard presents *Ninja Warrior UK* and says that everyone who comes on the programme looks attractive, whatever their age, because they are so fit. Even though some of them are in their fifties and sixties and have wrinkles galore, they still look amazing because they are in such good shape. They've got a spring in their step, a flexibility that instantly makes them seem younger. A lot of the wrinkle-free people I've met in Los

Angeles have the same sort of bounce, because they work out like crazy trying to get their bodies to match their faces.

I decided to go for it. OK, I thought, there are 168 hours in the week and I just need to do something vaguely energetic for anything between two and a half and five of those, according to the latest medical advice. That would leave me 163 hours to do everything else. Surely I could manage it?

My friend Penny Stokes-Hilton used to go at her fitness training like a total maniac after she'd dropped the children off at school. Only, instead of going to the gym, she'd come home and spend thirty whirlwind minutes clearing away the breakfast things, tidying the kids' rooms, scrubbing the outside steps, putting a wash on, changing sheets, dusting and vacuuming. 'It always made me feel great afterwards, because the house was tidy and I'd had a workout,' she said. 'Then the rest of the day was clear to get on with work and all the other things a busy mum crams into school hours.'

A note of warning, though: some studies into the effectiveness of housework as exercise have concluded that it isn't a vigorous enough activity to count as part of your two and a half hours. Knowing Penny as I do, I think in her case it would, but you must judge for yourself when it comes to your own domestic routine, as I'm not sure mine would measure up!

Another note of warning. Every day, there's a shock new statistic about national obesity. Conversely, there are a lot of articles written by people complaining about prejudice towards fat people. It's a complex debate and I believe that everyone's view should be respected, but in a chapter about health, it's probably important to say that having too much weight on you may prove to be an obstacle to getting fit. If it isn't, that's great. If it is, try to do whatever you can to get rid of the weight that is holding you back. Heart disease, high blood sugar leading to diabetes, high blood pressure leading to strokes, breathlessness, joint and back pain, and low self-esteem are some of the complications linked with being overweight. None of these make you feel in the least bit fabulous. Exercise is a great way to combat them.

But where to start?

'The gym works for me,' said my friend Rob Rinder, star of ITV's *Judge Rinder*. 'I get a trainer to devise me a routine and push myself as hard as I can in as quick a time as possible. It gets rid of all my stresses and gets me fit in one fell swoop.'

Considering how he wowed the nation with his toned torso and super-fitness in *Strictly Come Dancing* last year, Rob is a great advert for some gym action.

For me, there was always the dream that tomorrow I would go to the gym and get those walnut buttocks I've always longed for. But at forty-nine, the prospect of a rock-hard bottom seemed impossible, a battle lost before it had even started. I tried to imagine myself pumping iron and pounding the treadmill, but the very idea felt intimidating.

Also, I have a tendency to overdo things and I didn't want to risk any injuries.

I had to remind myself of what happened when I did *Strictly Come Dancing.* Unlike Rob, I was obviously a disaster at dancing, but taking part and doing that much exercise meant that, as the weeks went on, I felt amazing, because I had a sense of being in charge of my body for the first time ever – even though you wouldn't have seen any evidence of that on the dance floor! It didn't start out well, though. My first dance was the quickstep and I went into it with full gusto, as an innocent, unfit, enthusiastic thirty-nine-year-old, jumping and bouncing around continuously for a week. Then I woke up one morning and couldn't move my feet.

I could almost hear my inflamed tendons shrieking, 'What do you think you've been doing? You've stretched us once in the last year and now you've done it a thousand times a day for the last week. We cannot cope with it!'

So my new fitness regime now began with a power walk twice a week. I'd get to the school gates for pick-up forty-five minutes early, beg a favour of the receptionist to leave my bag and heavy laptop behind the desk as I'd come straight from work (no point in making it too hard!), whack on some trainers and headphones, and walk like a demon, singing loudly all the way – for twenty minutes in one direction and twenty minutes back. I tried to walk fast enough that I was a little out of breath and sweating, to raise my heart rate. I most likely looked bonkers, but my hope was that it would give me a sense of well-being that would then nudge me into more strenuous activities as I gradually built up my fitness levels. I wasn't aiming to become Triathlon Woman – I just wanted to be healthy and fit.

I guess that's everyone's aim, really. We all want to live as long as possible, and that's especially the case when we turn fifty, because we think, hey, we're a long way into our three score years and ten! Let's just extend this as much as we possibly can.

But in trying to live longer we sometimes don't focus enough on the things which will improve our quality of life as we age too. So, yes, doing exercise to improve our heart and lung health and invigorate our system is good, because that will help us to live longer. But we should also think about exercise that strengthens our joints and keeps us flexible, too. Is it so fantastic to live to a hundred if the final twenty years are marked by pain, or immobility? OK, we want to avoid a big death and live as long as we can, but we also want to live well. It's like an over-indulgent, overly long movie – just because it's three hours long does not necessarily make the last hour brilliant.

Woody Allen famously said, 'You can live to be a hundred if you give up all the things that make you want to live to be a hundred.' But it's more than that. There is no point rushing at a new exercise regime for the sake of it, because we want to achieve some mega body, and damaging our joints or straining our backs in the process, setting ourselves up for misery and incapacity in the future. So we need to find a balance of exercise that's right for each of us individually. I needed Rob's help to get mine right.

'OK, now you've got yourself moving, what do you really want to focus on?' Rob asked me.

I didn't know where to start. Thighs, abs, knees, upper arms – what *didn't* I want to focus on?

'I'd like to put a spring in my step,' I said, eventually.

'Ah, well, if you want spring and bounce, you need good joints, bones and muscles,' he said. 'You have to work on the areas that keep you moving, because mobility is essential to energising your heart and brain.

'You need to reinforce the muscles around your joints, build up your chest, back and abdomen to develop your core strength, think about your posture, eat calcium and protein-rich foods, and take vitamin D supplements.'

'Is the gym the only place I can do it?'

'If you're chickening out of the gym, you could try swimming instead.'

'Hey,' I said, 'I am not chickening out – just making a reasoned choice, honest.'

'Good,' he said, with a grin. 'Swimming will strengthen your joints, build your core muscles and tone your upper arms into the bargain. Although it will play havoc with your blowdry – so you'll have to cope with that!'

'Hmm, thanks.'

Rob knew how much confidence a trip to the hairdresser could give me. A good, bouncy blowdry always makes me feel as if I can take on the world – rather like Cheryl Cole, now known as just Cheryl, who once told me, 'The bigger the hair, the closer to God, I always say!'

But Rob had also heard me moan about my floppy bingo wings often enough, too. I was longing to be able to wear sleeveless evening dresses with confidence again, particularly as these days there seemed to be fewer and fewer options for which bits of my body I could reveal on nights out. Debbie Harper, our Head of Wardrobe at *Good Morning Britain*, was always telling me, 'You can't cover everything up, Kate! Where's the sizzle in that?!'

It seems to me that clothes are designed in three ways for nights out: a short hem with your top covered; a long hem, with lots of cleavage; or sleeveless and elegant, like Audrey Hepburn. Unlike my friend and *GMB* colleague, Charlotte Hawkins, who has legs that would make Bambi's look stumpy, mine have always been rather 'pit pony' – functional but not very foal-like – so I have never been drawn to uber-short for the red carpet. And, at forty-nine, after two kids, I wasn't sure I could get away with the slashed-to-the-waist, low-cut, boobs-out look any more, either. That left me with either the covered top-to-toe shroud look, or braving sleeveless and elegant, for which I needed some serious upper arm toning.

For some reason, my kids are fascinated by ageing upper arms. They say to my mother, 'Granny, shake your arm. Wow, look at that! It's amazing!'

'Don't,' I remonstrate. 'Granny might find it a bit awkward.' (Although Granny doesn't appear to mind flapping her arms at all.)

'Mum, your arms are starting to go like Granny's!' Billy cried gleefully, a few months ago.

Something had to be done.

'Find something you can do in the odd moments in your day that will keep you toned,' advised the super-fit Susanna Reid. 'I love the gym, but there is no point in paying a fortune in gym membership if you're not going to find the time to go. And there are apps that give you five-, seven- or ten-minute workouts – and just use whatever is handy as weights.'

Water bottles are perfect and they force you to drink more, which is also good. So I started carrying around two Evian bottles in my bag. It put my shoulder out slightly, but at least I could do arm-sculpting exercises whenever I had five minutes to spare. When no one was looking, I'd stand feet apart, arms straight at my sides, with a bottle in each hand. Then I'd raise my arms diagonally into a V-shape until they were parallel to the floor, almost as if I were stretching them out to hug someone, and hold for a few seconds before lowering them back down to my sides. Easy.

Actually, it worked. The only thing is, you have to keep doing it – and my problem was that I kept on drinking the water, which either messed up the weight distribution (one bottle full and the other half-empty, fiddling about trying to pour water from one into the other) or just meant I was lifting virtually empty plastic bottles, which was pointless. Also, the sound team who miked me up in the morning kept on thinking I wanted a hug. They would open the dressing room door, ready to clip on the battery packs and cables that we wear for *Good Morning Britain*, see me coming towards them with my arms outstretched, and come over and give me a hug, saying, 'Oh, Kate, it's good to see you too!' Which, although delightful, rather interrupted things, and made me look seriously needy. Lorraine and Glenn, I do love you, but perhaps not as much as it has appeared over the last few weeks!

The exercise apps were also freaking out my colleagues a bit. 'Er, are you OK?' asked Dave Brierley-Jones, my producer at Smooth Radio, when I started doing arm dips and press-ups while we were on-air. 'Hotel California' by the Eagles was playing – six minutes, forty-eight seconds – which I judged perfect for a five-minute upper body workout.

'Just using my time effectively. Have you tried it?'

Before long, he was joining in as well. The Smooth studio is in the same building as a load of other radio stations, like Capital and Heart, and the walls between them are made of glass, so we can see the other presenters who are on-air at the same time, doing their thing in their studios. My old *Daybreak* mate, Aled Jones, who was on-air on Classic FM in the studio right next to mine, spotted the activity and rushed to join in during one of his long symphonies. Then Andrew Castle, who was passing by on the way to present his LBC show, saw what was going on. Ever the competitive sportsman, he came in and started trying to outdo Aled and Dave in the number of one-handed press-ups he could complete in a minute. It was so chaotic that I nearly missed the end of the song and had to rush to the mic before we ended up with silence, or 'dead air', which is obviously a big no-no in radio. Still, at least I was having fun with exercise and managing to squeeze it into my working day!

To improve my flexibility, I figured I needed to stretch. 'Yoga, yoga, yoga,' said my friend, broadcaster and author Penny Smith, who used to work with me at *GMTV*. 'As you get older, the wrong things are getting soft and the wrong things are getting stiff. You need to keep flexible to keep moving. And yoga is the perfect way to do that.'

'Really, yoga?' I said with a sigh of defeat.

Penny loves yoga. She'd happily hang out all day in a pair of billowy trousers eating beansprouts and balancing on her head. But she is also a very good mate of mine and looks spectacularly great for fifty-whatever-it-is – or 'thirty-seven, recurring', as she always puts it. So any advice she had to offer was definitely worth listening to. 'If you can't do yoga as often as me,' she said, 'keep up the swimming and have a deep-tissue massage every now and then. That'll do it.'

I have always thought of massages as a total luxury – to be saved for a birthday treat or a hen night spa day. So I loved the idea they could be a healthy essential. In fact, a good deep-tissue massage will soften the fibrous fascia around your muscles in the same way that yoga does, allowing them to move more easily. It can alleviate the problems caused by injury, inflammation and chronic stress, and loosen your neck muscles and hamstrings, giving you back some of the youthful flexibility you might have thought was lost for good. It's not a luxury, then. If you haven't got time for yoga, a good massage therapist is the next best thing.

While I was thinking about getting a spring in my step, I flashed back to my *Strictly Come Dancing* days again. Once the tendonitis had got better and my dancing improved, the crew started telling me how great I was looking.'You don't realise it, but you're like a different person,' said Darren, the lovely cameraman who used to bring me chocolates every morning. 'You look so much younger because you're walking tall.'

Now, this came down to my posture, which I think is genuinely important. As you age, you shrink and slump. Of course, some people can't avoid it because they get arthritis or osteoporosis. But generally, it seems that holding yourself properly and having good posture is as much the key to feeling loose and limber as pumping iron in the gym.

You wouldn't think that posture was something you could find, only to lose it again. But I'd lost mine – and I wanted it back, especially as I was starting to get aches in my spine. My friend Chris Hawkins, a presenter on BBC Radio 6 Music, recommended the Alexander Technique and it was revolutionary. This wasn't only because it made me mindful of my posture, balance and co-ordination, which enabled me to make a dramatic difference to the way I moved and walked. It was also because it helped me feel more relaxed, by releasing muscular tension in my body that contributed to my bad posture – tension that might well have been hanging around for decades, possibly even from childhood.

At the heart of the technique is the idea of having a string that runs through your body from the top of your head, and another from your navel to your spine. There are lots of accessible books and websites about it, but Chris recommended a teacher called Sandra who lived near to the kids' school, so I could pop into her house for a session before school pick-up.

In our first session, Sandra watched me move and assessed some of the basic mistakes I was making. A lot of the time I wasn't standing with my weight evenly distributed. There was constant tension in my shoulder. The relationship between my neck, shoulders and back was slightly askew. 'If you carry on like this,' she said, 'you're going to get more and more backache.'

In the lessons that followed, Sandra taught me to hold myself in a way that relaxed both my neck and shoulders. This required a certain mindfulness that had a calming effect on my mind as well as my body. It was really interesting. I'm not saying I won't slump again – I'm simply not aware enough of what I'm doing half the time – but the lessons had a profound effect on me and started a process of change that I don't think will reverse. I'm not going to lose my posture again. I'm determined.

'Have you noticed a difference in your brain since you started getting fit?' my super-fit friend Julia asked me, a few weeks after I'd started my new regime.

This was something I wasn't sure about. Maybe I *was* thinking more clearly, but I was tired so much of the time that it was hard to tell. What I'd really noticed was that my mood was better. I felt good about addressing my posture and getting my body moving. It lifted my self-esteem.

However, I was still forgetting people's names halfway through a conversation and I was also having the kind of crazy lapses in concentration that ended with discovering my belt in the fridge and the milk on the chest of drawers. Go upstairs, what have I come here for? Go downstairs, oh yes, now I remember. Go upstairs, what was it again? Expletive, expletive, expletive.

'How do I sharpen up my brain?' I wailed to my producer Dave at Smooth. Earlier that morning, I'd come out of the house to take the kids to school, only to realise that I'd parked the car halfway across London the day before.

He smiled at me and I sensed that he was going to say something ironic. 'Listen to more music,' he said sweetly.

Ironic, but right on the money. Because music activates deep structures in the brain and exercises crucial areas of your cerebrum, which have to work hard to make sense of the relationships between notes, beats and rhythms. Whether it's an Abba track or a Brahms concerto, music is a complex cypher of sounds that our brains enjoy decoding. I took my job at Smooth Radio partly because I felt there wasn't enough music in my life, and I'm glad I did, because it's been brilliant.

When researchers at Johns Hopkins University persuaded jazz and rap musicians to lie inside an MRI scanner and improvise, they saw a lot of brain matter light up on their monitors, proof that music gets your brain processing madly, like a happy computer. It works on many different levels and, like smell, triggers instant recall. You hear a snatch of Bowie's 'Wild is the Wind' and you're transported back to dancing in the Côte d'Azur moonlight with that gorgeous man you thought you were going to marry (what a rat he turned out to be!) just like it was yesterday. Two bars of the intro to 'Summer Nights' and you're in your childhood bedroom with seven of your best girlfriends from school, yelling and screeching along to the *Grease* soundtrack.

It's a kind of therapy, isn't it, when every song from your past seems to set off a mini-catharsis. Nostalgia, a sense of loss, a blast of teenage summer excitement, ruefulness, the feeling that you've made it through to the other side of heartbreak ... You can feel it doing you good, even if it makes you spit.

Listening to old favourites is one thing – and I feel really lucky that I get to relive my teens and twenties every day on my radio show – but there's increasing evidence that listening to new music really gets the synapses fizzing. Trying to decode a new song, especially one that jars at first, is double exercise for the brain as it struggles to make sense of unfamiliar sounds. It also opens you up to new influences, even if you decide to reject them, which keeps you fresh.

Great, I'm in the right job, then. 'But I've still got a bit of a sluggish brain,' I told my friend Joel, who is a medical researcher. 'And the name thing is really getting to me. I can't be forgetting what elder statesmen are called halfway through interviewing them.'

'I've cut my drinking right down,' he said. 'It's made a big difference to my clarity of thought.'

I don't drink very much these days, but it's still nice to know that a study at the University of Sydney concluded that exercise may well counteract the deadlier effects of alcohol. The problem is, you feel the effects of alcohol so much more as you get older. The last time I got drunk was at the *TV Choice* awards. It was a brilliant, ridiculous evening and I giggled and danced all night, but I was still in pain three days later.

I don't drink because I'm always getting up early and there's nothing worse than waking up with a hangover and a child jumping on the bed, all bright-eyed and bushy-tailed. Also, I'm now of an age when I think about the next-day consequences of the next glass of wine at nine the night before, while I'm actually drinking. It ruins the fun to think, no, those after-effects are too unbearable. And I've decided that if I can't have the fun, I'm not having the pain. Well, not often anyway!

Coffee offers short-term alertness, but I tend to slump an hour after I've drunk a cup, which is no good, and I feel wired if I have any more than that. Drinking lots of water is meant to be good for the brain. It's boring, but I think being hydrated is a good idea. It makes a massive difference to your skin and boosts your brain's reaction time, according to a study at the University of East London. You don't necessarily have to drink two and a half litres a day obsessively, but a refreshing, tall glass of water two or three times a day will do you the world of good.

'Why don't you try using a brain app?' Joel suggested. 'Lots of people I know are into Lumosity and CogniFit.'

OK, a brain app. Move over, sudoku. It hadn't occurred to me that I could download an application on to my phone that would provide games to improve my mental skills. This opened me up to exercises developed by neuroscientists to improve cognitive abilities like memory and concentration. Yippee! I downloaded three and played them manically over a weekend. Did they work? Again, I'm not sure, but they were certainly addictive. I started to wonder if they were just 'another thing to do' in this crazy busy world of short attention spans, so I deleted them and downloaded a couple of mindfulness apps. Headspace is a good one. I also liked Walking Meditations and used it for a couple of brisk walks in the park.

'Why don't you just read a good novel?' my mum said. 'You've always loved reading.'

Well, scientists say that reading novels improves brain function and connectivity, de-stresses you, strengthens your analytical skills, stimulates the imagination and encourages empathy, among other things. So Mum was right – and I went straight out and bought the latest Sebastian Faulks novel (love him!).

When I discussed all this with Ben Shephard, he had another idea for me. 'Silence is incredibly important,' he said.

Hmmm. I pushed aside the thought that he just wanted me to shut up for five minutes, because I could see he was right. At fifty you have very little silence in your life. You're either on the phone, or with your kids, or someone's got the telly on, or there's music or chatter in the background. Maybe silence also means emotional space, which is important at all ages but seems to happen quite naturally at a younger age. You have lie-ins in your twenties on your own on a Saturday morning and without realising it you're thinking your own thoughts.

There is scientific evidence that daydreaming, or letting your mind wander, is good for you. Too much noise can damage our brains, while silence has been proven to restore cognitive function, reduce stress, replenish attention levels and regenerate brain cells in mice.

What about vitamins? I'm a fan. Which ones are good for the brain? At my local health shop, they recommended vitamin B6, B12 and folic acid, along with ginkgo biloba, rosemary, sage and omega-3.

'Vitamins, shmitamins,' said my Smooth producer Dave, who doesn't believe anything that hasn't been scientifically proven. 'Stop wasting your money. You can get all the nutrients you need from your diet.'

Is that actually true? I know that several studies have concluded that there's no benefit to taking a daily multivitamin, but are they saying that women with low iron and calcium levels shouldn't top them up? Many women of menopausal age take calcium to try and prevent osteoporosis. What about the NHS guidelines that now say we should consider boosting our vitamin D levels with supplements, because it can be hard to get enough (10 micrograms) from our diet? Joint specialists recommend taking omega-3 and glucosamine sulphate, and a lot of people with arthritis swear by rosehip.

The fact is, I believe in supplements. That's partly because, when I was trying to have a baby and taking all those pro-fertile vitamins they sell at Boots, I noticed a difference in my hair and nails. It is also partly because a Maasai medicine man once told me that supplements were the only part of Western medicine that we get right.

'I see,' said Dave, his eyes glittering with amusement. 'I'm guessing you don't want to live in a hut, paint yourself in powder or have your son circumcised in a tent with a knife, but ...'

'Look, this is a piece of Maasai advice I agree with – and that's good enough for me.'

We laughed about my disregard for science and logic, but I still think vitamins can help, no matter what the studies say – and millions of people clearly feel the same way. Vitamins are a multi-million dollar business. Just make sure you get yours from a reputable source, because there's a lot of sawdust out there, especially if you order online.

There's a vitamin for everything, of course. If you believed all the hype, you could end up swallowing a sack load every day, like my friend Vickie who started taking herbal supplements like they were going out of fashion when she hit her forties. 'I'm getting aches,' she wailed. 'It's the start of old age and I'm chucking money at it.'

A bit of background about Vickie: she is uber-glamorous. Her view is that if it's a choice between comfort and glamour, it should always be glamour. Everything about her is feminine and glittery. Her hair is blonde and used to be backcombed to the point where we were going to a wedding once and she physically couldn't get in the taxi, because her hair was so high. Seriously!

One day Vickie woke up with a terrible backache and went to the doctor, who said, 'It's muscular. I think you should try a sports massage.'

She paid a fortune for this sports massage. Apparently, the practitioner said, 'Yes, everything is majorly out of line and you've got the beginnings of a hump.'

She rang me up afterwards, hysterical. 'I'm getting a hump!' she shrieked. 'Oh my God, what's the vitamin for that?'

You've gotta love her.

'Would that be the stand-up-straight vitamin?' I said. 'I really don't know.'

So I think you can go down a road of trying everything, when in fact all she really needed was a physio and a daily programme of exercises. She's right as rain now and her hair is bouncier and higher than ever, so all is well with the world.

Meanwhile, my mother, buoyed by her clever piece of advice about reading novels, decided to weigh in again. 'Your real problem is that you don't get enough sleep,' she observed sagely, as only mothers can.

She was right again, sigh. 'Remember the lead-up to the referendum on Europe?' she said.

How could I forget? I was abroad three nights a week, working ridiculous hours, going live at six in the morning and filming until eleven at night. I was literally counting the minutes of sleep.

Two days after the referendum results, I said to Derek, 'I think I'm losing my mind. I'm genuinely worried about my brain. I cannot physically think.'

The kids were noticing too. My ten-year-old kept yelling, 'Mum, you're not listening! You're staring into space.' You of course have to be well rested to be present and functional with the kids, and I definitely wasn't.

'You are exhausted,' Derek said. 'You've got to stop – stop thinking and stop doing.' Fortunately we were going away for a few days with his mum and dad, who are brilliant at looking after the kids and letting me rest.

I can't remember the first three days of the holiday, other than the fact that they were lovely. I was zonked out. I slept for twelve hours each night – and by the fourth day I felt more normal, or at least as if I could have a conversation with someone.

I'm notorious among my friends for existing on no sleep. I used to work like crazy pre-kids, and party and not sleep properly or just sleep erratically. Then I'd go on holiday with the girls and flop. It came to a zenith the time we all went to Dubai. We were really excited and had a lovely time on the plane chatting. Then the others nodded off but I didn't go to sleep because I was too wired and I love movies on planes. We landed quite late, zipped along to the hotel and went to bed.

Everyone was up bright and early the next morning, except me. 'She'll be having a lie-in, she's knackered,' they decided and went to breakfast. After breakfast, they went down to the beach, lazed in the sun, had lunch. When they came back from the beach at four that afternoon, I had still not emerged and wasn't answering my phone. Is she OK? they wondered. They started to worry a little bit.

At seven o'clock, they decided to get a key for my room. 'What if she is actually dead?' they asked each other.

When they entered my room, I was lying motionless, curled up like a little mouse. I was so absolutely still that they put a mirror to my mouth to check I was breathing. There was a kerfuffle and I woke up and said, 'Hi! Sorry, I promise I'll get up in a minute.'

'No problem,' they said, relieved. 'We were worried that you'd slept too long.'

They went downstairs and had dinner – and I went on sleeping all through the night and into the morning, when I finally woke up. It was a thirty-two-hour marathon recharge, proving that I actually do need to sleep!

These days, I can do a few nights in a row of three or four hours' sleep, but go beyond that and my brain just shuts down. It probably was always like that, except that I had so much youthful energy I could compensate. Now my cut-off is six hours: if I can get six hours' sleep I can function – but anything less is a struggle.

As the journalist and businesswoman, Arianna Huffington, points out, 'The irony is that a lot of people forego sleep in the name of productivity. But in fact our productivity is reduced substantially when we're sleep deprived.'

Whereas once you used to go into work and boast about how little sleep you'd had the night before, now you brag about how much sleep you've had. Well, some people do – and I wish I could.

Quite often as I'm going to bed, I look at the clock and think, oh dear, even if I fall asleep this second, I'm only going to have four and a half hours' sleep.

It can be very easy to panic, which is totally counter-productive. So I say to myself, it's going to be fine. Go to sleep. It's better than nothing. I'm going to feel rubbish when I wake up, but it will be just enough to pep me up and it's going to be OK.

I'm really kind to myself when I wake up. I always have a shower and give myself some time to get used to the day. I'm lucky not to have to drive myself into work – I have someone picking me up so I can sit and stare into space on the journey – and when I leave work, I'm very single-minded about getting some rest. I get in the car, check the driver will be taking the quickest route and say, 'Could you wake me up when we're five minutes from home?' Then I curl up, or put the seat back, force myself not to think about anything and sleep for the next forty minutes. It's just long enough to refresh me.

Isn't it annoying that no one can be in three places at once! Sometimes I'll be working on a show at the weekend – maybe the BBC's *National Lottery* or ITV's *The Xtra Factor*, both of which I love doing – but I'll also be asked to a show or a party that I should really go to if I don't want to offend anyone. Sometimes that will mean being out both nights of a weekend, away from the kids and Derek, when I'm really knackered and need two days of flop time with my family. It's always a dilemma, but I'm getting better at turning things down, thankfully. More and more, I am realising that I need my sleep, and my kids and my husband close.

I think my conclusion, when talking about health, is that it's important to make healthy choices that are right for you. For me, that has started to mean eating well, working to keep my bounce and flexibility, making sure I do something that gets my heart really pumping three times a week and getting enough sleep. Those things seemed to be working for me. Until someone mentioned the dreaded spectre of the menopause, that is, which threatened to throw everything up in the air.

CHAPTER 8

Slaying the Menopause Monster

'You are utterly not qualified to write about midlife!' my friend Vickie spluttered. 'You've never even had a grey pubic hair.'

'My God,' I said, recoiling. 'Am I going to get grey pubes?'

She sighed in exasperation. 'You see? *And* grey eyebrows.'

Gawd! I spend so much time getting rid of the grey hair on my head that I didn't stop to think that was coming too.

'And since you haven't got any symptoms of menopause, you don't really know the full panic,' she added.

'True,' I said. 'I haven't had any hot flushes. My periods still seem regular. But my skin is drier, definitely.'

'That's it? You're forty-nine and all you've got is dry skin?' she howled.

'I thought fifty-one was the average age for menopause in the UK?'

'Yes, but haven't you heard of the perimenopause? The menopause's little sister? Its oh-so-hilarious warm-up act? There are about fifty potential symptoms of the perimenopause alone.'

'I don't want to talk about this any more,' I said.

'Fine. Bury your head in the sand. But you're not going to be able to avoid it, because it's coming at you.'

The next day on Smooth, the producers were celebrating because a major skincare company had approached us about sponsoring my show. It's great when a sponsor gets involved, not least because they nearly always offer listeners the chance to win a big prize – in this case, a luxury spa break. It's good for the station and it shows great faith in the show as well. When announcing details of the competition, the company offering the prize gets a mention too.

In this case, we had to explain that the firm behind the prize were specialists in 'expert skincare for women during the menopause'. I looked around at my team of twenty-year-old lads. They looked distinctly uncomfortable. Let's be honest – boys don't really like talking about periods, and I suspected they liked hearing about them stopping even less. 'Do I actually have to use the word menopause? It's not very glamorous, is it?!' I ventured. 'Can't I just say "women of a certain age" or "women in their prime"?'

The team explained it had to be 'menopause' because the company wanted to reach out to the women who are looking for help at this specific time. Their philosophy was that if you are in the middle of the menopause, it's dominating your thoughts and you are looking for anything to relieve it. So you tune into the word – it actually attracts you.

'But surely it will repel everyone else?!' I wailed.

Then an awful thought struck me – it was actually an entirely reasonable request from them, and I was the one being unreasonable. Why was I, a 49-year-old woman, recoiling at this being attached to my show? Shouldn't I be embracing the idea? What on earth was going on?

I went to meet my friend Helen Warner for lunch. 'We naturally shy away from discussing the menopause because it signifies all the negative things about being middle aged,' she said over salad and chips. 'The end of fertility, getting old, losing your looks, becoming invisible ... You stop feeling like a vibrant, sexy woman.'

I nodded dolefully, wondering whether I should just book a flight to Thailand, swim out to sea and wait for a shark to eat me.

'But actually it doesn't have to be that way at all,' she added.

'Phew, that's a relief,' I said, mentally swimming back to land.

You hear so many horror stories. People talk about ten years of sweating, anxiety, palpitations, heavy periods, dryness, dragging tiredness, brain fog, depression, sleep disorder, headaches, joint stiffness, osteoporosis and plummeting sex drive. Kill me now. My mum says she kept forgetting words. It doesn't bear thinking about.

Some people breeze through it, but you don't meet them very often, do you? Or maybe they just don't talk about it because they don't want to seem smug.

So, what actually happens during the menopause? With all those unspeakable symptoms to contend with, it's easy to feel that you're under attack from your body. But actually it's a natural process; it is not a disease or a disorder. We are born with a finite number of eggs and once we've used them up, our ovaries shut down and our periods stop, after which we're unable to have any more babies. At the same time our hormone levels begin to fluctuate – especially our oestrogen, which drops off a cliff as our ovaries stop working – and that's what causes all the havoc.

Apparently there's still a lot we don't know, including why we get it, what exactly happens and the best way to treat it. Hey, we don't really know anything about the menopause! It's the biggest hormonal shift we'll experience since adolescence and nobody seems to know what it's for.

Great.

The only other animals that experience menopause are whales, so we don't have much to compare ourselves to. There's a theory that women live on after our reproductive life has ended because Nature values the nurturing qualities of grandmothers. Can that be true? Clearly grannies are lovely. They dole out advice and famously knit fabulous jumpers, and these days, let's be honest, are relied on more and more by the working mums among us for 'grannycare'. But are they really necessary for the survival of the species? Another theory – perhaps more credible – is that giving birth is difficult enough for creatures who walk upright and have small pelvises, so it's best done when you're young enough to have a fighting chance of survival on your own in a cave while the rest of the tribe is off foraging for berries. Otherwise you might die. Better not risk it.

What's interesting is that just a hundred years ago, women routinely expired in their forties, before they even went through menopause – and those who made it to 'the change' saw it as a depressing signifier of the imminent slide towards death. But now, more than ten million people in the UK are female and over fifty, and many of them can expect to live into their eighties. That's thirty years that a lot of women didn't have before – three extra decades of life! Subsequently a whole new section of society has emerged, a swathe of post-fifty women whose energies aren't focused on childrearing. It still doesn't answer the question of how the menopause fits into Nature's plan, but it's pretty seismic. You can view it as a whole new evolutionary group.

Although it would be nice to know why Nature puts women through this cataclysmic change, what really matters is getting through it OK. How do you make it to that place where those at the forefront of post-menopausal life fizz and sparkle away, full of verve and energy? I'm thinking of women like Dame Helen Mirren, Angela Merkel, Theresa May and Oprah Winfrey.

The only solution I can see is to get out there and talk about it to women who have been through it. Work the grapevine, listen to the jungle drums. Fortunately HRT worked for my mum and a couple of my mates said it totally saved them, so there's always that option. But not everyone can take HRT and it doesn't always work, plus it's not entirely safe. According to the latest research, taking combined HRT (oestrogen and progesterone) is associated with a small increased risk of breast cancer and oestrogen-only HRT can increase the risk of endometrial cancer.

If you're suffering, it is crucial to find a sympathetic GP and talk over your options. Some people don't like the idea that HRT is synthetically processed and prefer to take bioidentical HRT derived from plants like yam and soy. You may have to pay quite hefty consulting fees if you go this route, and you should talk to others who have tried it first. One of my mates found that bio-identical hormones worked brilliantly. Another took them for seven months without much effect. 'Finally, I caved in,' she told me. 'I slapped an HRT patch on my arm and felt better within twenty-four hours.'

Whatever it is you're going through, you can be sure that someone else has had it worse and blogged their recovery programme. Even though not everything you read will be useful, this is one of the wonders of the internet, so take advantage of it. Supplements seem to have helped many people through their symptoms. Among the most popular is red clover, which contains isoflavones and plant oestrogen and is said to help balance hormones. Some people swear by magnesium to sharpen the brain. The newsreader, Carol Barnes, has written about how sage capsules helped banish her hot flushes and sweating, and she went on taking sage post-menopause as a memory booster. Black cohosh, passionflower and chasteberry are constantly being mentioned. The British Homeopathic Association reports great success with treating menopause. Traditional Chinese Herbal Medicine has a range of remedies too. But of course a lot of people don't believe in this kind of stuff.

Diet and nutrition are obviously key – and a study by the Royal College of Obstetricians and Gynaecologists found that regular aerobic exercise can help relieve menopausal symptoms. Numerous other studies back up these findings. In fact, it seems as if everything that has been written about the menopause in the past decade says that exercise is one of the best remedies.

My friend Helen Warner has a really positive story about how taking on an exercise regime helped her sister-in-law, Helen Duggan, through menopause. 'She went from being the lowest she had ever been to feeling happy, healthy and sexy. She looks amazing now. She's suddenly wearing mini-skirts! She's loving it.'

Helen Duggan has written a blog about how she went through a surgical menopause after she had her ovaries removed in 2016. The operation laid her low. She had to stop exercising and seriously curtail her social life. As she recovered, instead of feeling rejuvenated after years of suffering ovarian cysts, she lost her spark, felt depressed and her self-esteem hit the floor – classic menopausal symptoms. A massive fitness fan, she was desperate to get back to the gym, but a nurse advised her to remember she was fifty and take it easy. As if. And if this wasn't annoying enough, two years earlier, a neurologist had advised her to pack in the gym and try picking up a book, for the same reason.

Helen was prescribed HRT and subsequently anti-depressants to combat her horrendous symptoms, but they just got worse. She became ever more miserable, absent-minded and dizzy, plagued by hot flushes and insomnia. 'I was at my lowest ebb,' she says. 'You just don't realise how big the menopause is until it happens to you. I was certainly not prepared at all.'

Finally she found a sympathetic GP who told her to throw away the medication, which was obviously not helping. 'Stop taking it and let's see what happens,' she said.

Helen was overjoyed. 'It was music to my ears and I wondered why I hadn't thought of it myself.'

Helen gave herbal remedies a try next, and acupuncture. She tried to return to running but kept getting injured. Whenever she Googled her latest injury, everything pointed to her age and the menopause. 'I was panic-stricken. Was this the end of exercise for me? Would I have to give up the one thing that had kept me mentally strong for two decades?'

Thankfully, she found John Reynolds, a soft-tissue and biomechanics expert who showed her how to strengthen her body and mind using exercise, yoga, cold-water therapy (in its simplest form, this means having cold showers and baths), stretching and rest.

His motto – and now hers – is, 'If your core is strong, you can do anything.' These days she's at the gym every day, goes on regular parkruns and even runs 10K races.

'From my experience, you can turn this period of turbulence into a positive and become a stronger person,' she says, beaming. 'I actually feel better than I did before the menopause – I faced it head on and turned it into something great. To other women, I would say, don't listen to the negativity. Our bodies can be as strong and capable as ever at fifty, if we treat them properly. It's definitely not time for granny knickers and a blue rinse just yet.'

Now as you know, I love big knickers, but the blue rinse was never going to flatter my skin tone, so I was glad it could wait. Inspired, I decided to up my half hour power walk to a bit of jogging too. Just very gently around the park for thirty minutes at a time. All the articles I've read about the menopause recommend a combination of strength, flexibility and aerobic exercise, so I'm also planning to go swimming every Wednesday and pump up the tyres on my bike. That counts, doesn't it – pumping up tyres? Oh God, my children will probably insist I ride the blooming thing too.

Or perhaps I'll be more like my friend Penny Stokes-Hilton – the big sister I never had – when my symptoms kick in, if they do. She says it's important to accept that your body is changing. 'There are two types of women

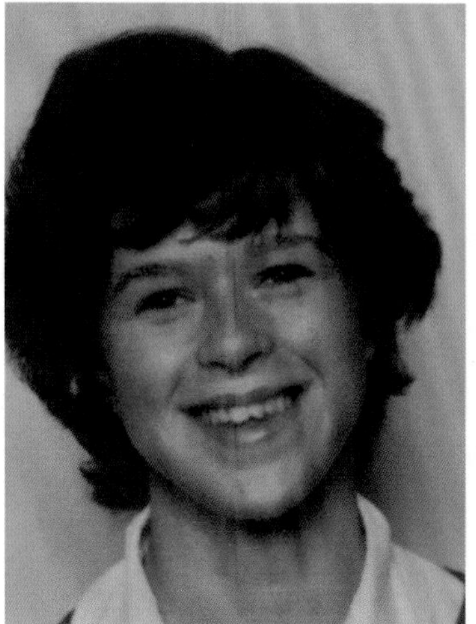

Not a 'natural looker', or a natural blonde!

Formative years, just starting out. I look so young!

Me after a year of eating forbidden fruits!

My lovely husband

My super-glam mum, super brother Matthew, and super-fit dad – surfing at 81!

My fabulous best friends

My gorgeous boss at ITV, Helen Warner

Keeping warm at President Donald Trump's Inauguration in Washington (thanks heated knickers!)

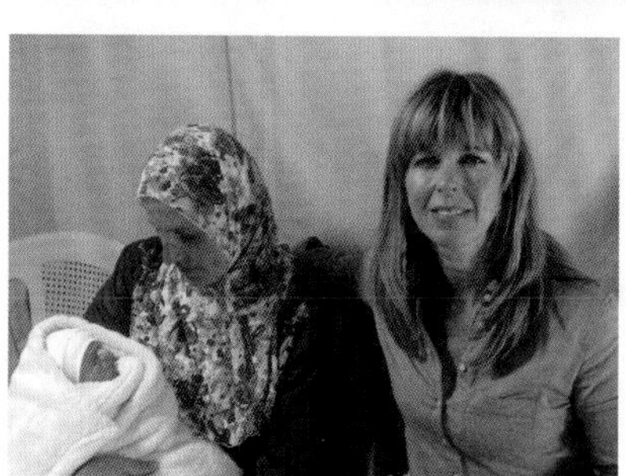

Gaining perspective, reporting from a refugee camp in 2013, on the Syrian border

Birthday fun at Smooth with Dave, my producer – my 49th birthday, NOT 50th!

Me, banished with my eggs!

Sneaking chocolates at work, and my fab *GMB* friends!

Being aged for a *GMB* story, above, and Paul and Pauline getting me ready for the ITV Gala

© Ken McKay/ITV/REX/Shutterstock

Embarrassing mishaps do happen on live TV – but why always to me?!

© ITV

© Ken McKay/ITV/REX/Shutterstock

Susanna Reid – always with me through the tough times, and the gang at the ITV Gala

Stars share their feel-good secrets...

when it comes to the menopause,' she says. 'There are those who try and fight it and stay as fit as they used to be, which is great. But that didn't work for me. I was the second type; I found I had to be much kinder to my body. If I felt tired, I took a rest. If I felt exhausted and depleted, I went for a massage. Eventually, I came through it, by taking care of myself and listening to my body. Now I feel renewed and refreshed.'

So there are lots of things you can do to mitigate the physical and mental symptoms of menopause. But, I wonder, is there anything that can help you feel better about losing your fertility? Because that's a hard one to let go, I think, and I've always had a massive problem with letting go of anything.

Still, if there's one thing that forces you to chuck out the old and get on with the new, it's moving house. So it was actually quite a good thing that we embarked on a cataclysmic uprooting in the year I was turning fifty. Suddenly I had two brilliant reasons to start afresh. Almost without thinking, in the weeks leading up to the move I started throwing away all but the tiniest things, even stuff I'd kept from my schooldays, allowing myself to hold on to just one thing from each era so that I didn't end up feeling as if I had no past. I felt a lot lighter afterwards.

The house I was leaving was the one I had moved to after going through an unbelievably heartbreaking divorce. It was where I'd made a fresh start, met my husband, Derek, and brought my babies home from the hospital to their new little room, which I'd decorated with 'The Teddy Bears' Picnic' themed curtains. It was where our wonderful world of family life opened up, so it was a very hard place to leave. It felt like a brutal end to an era, but I sensed that it was a good physical way of embracing fifty and beyond.

Still, I wasn't sure what to do with a photograph that had been taken for a magazine shoot ten years before, very late on in my first pregnancy with my daughter, Darcey. It had been up on the wall all these years – a sweet reminder of a special time – and as I was taking it down to pack it away, I looked at it more closely.

It was taken for *OK!* magazine and the editor had kindly sent me a framed copy around the time it appeared. There I am with an enormous round belly, lying on a bed in a tiny crop top, looking dreamily into space, oblivious of what's to come – the good, the bad and the life-changing – captured at the exact moment when a whole new chapter of my life is about to start. And I look so innocent.

I began to wrap it up in packing paper and found as I did that tears were flowing down my cheeks. Now that I'm turning fifty, I thought, that era of childbirth is gone. There's no way I'll go through it again.

The photograph marked the beginning of something. Taking it down was a kind of ending. It's a particularly poignant moment for a woman, I think – and there was added wistfulness in the fact that we were moving house and saying goodbye.

There was something else too. I had found it hard to accept that I wouldn't have a third child, partly because I'd had an idea in my mind that in having a third child I would become my mother, in the best possible way. My dream was to stop working, go to baby groups and make jam. When it didn't happen, I felt robbed, which was ludicrous and I feel guilty about that, considering that some people can't have any children at all. But at that point I didn't feel I'd finished, and that was as much to do with accepting that my life had gone in a certain direction as it was a desire for a third child. Instead of railing against fate, I needed to recognise that it had actually been the choices I'd made along the way that had led me to having children later in life. I had to accept that I'd made those choices for good reasons and there was no point in having regrets.

Of course, it isn't utterly impossible for a woman to have a child naturally at forty-nine. In fact, a small study at the University of Edinburgh has uncovered evidence that the human ovary may be able to grow new eggs in adulthood. The implications are huge. It means that in the future, older women might be able to conceive using their own eggs. But right now, for most people it's not possible at forty-nine, although that doesn't include men, obviously. Is this why men seem far less conscious of ageing than women? Men seem to think, oh God, I'm fifty, I haven't got enough time left to do all the things I want to do! They're concerned that their time is running out for fabulousness. They don't seem to feel the loss that we do and I'm sure it's to do with fertility and breeding. In theory, men stay fertile all their lives and they're programmed to fancy women who are fertile. But women aren't usually fertile after forty-five, so it's a double loss for us.

My feeling is that, although it's healthy to acknowledge that loss and the sadness around it, fifty is surely the perfect moment to move on. It seems a good time to take ownership of your past and make peace with the choices you've made and the things you've done. To think: I did this or that for a reason and I'm happy with it.

So I got rid of the cot and chucked out the baby car seat. I couldn't quite bring myself to give the pram away, but that's only because I want it to go to a good home, so I'm waiting for a friend or someone close to me to need one. Honest!

What about the photograph? Would I put it up in the new house, or was I taking it down for good? As I packed it up, I wondered whether I should I leave it behind, in a positive way, rather than harking back to the past.

Can I just let go? I thought. And if I do, will I instantly hurtle into the menopause maelstrom and start going bonkers?

I had to face the fact that as you grow older your place in the order of life changes, whether you have children or not – and that having a contented midlife meant accepting the new order, rather than fighting it. It's hard, because there's this amazing moment when you're a mum with a young baby and you're right at the core of a new beginning. Even if you're dying inside, if you're miserable and lonely, crying as you breast-feed, you're at the centre of your baby's world. Then suddenly things move on and you have this fantastic, visceral, energetic ball of energy pushing out into the world and pushing you away. The parent of a teenager is constantly reminded of how they're on the way out.

I felt this keenly when a pair of boots with a low heel (her first heel) arrived in the post for Darcey one morning – a cross between cowboy and biker boots, with studs on the side. She clomped up and down the hall holding a plastic box that she thinks looks like a briefcase and announced, 'I'm going to wear these on my first day at secondary school' (a year away). She was so excited about the boots, the future and life in general. Meanwhile, I was about to leave for work and as I walked down the stairs the heel of my favourite pair of shoes broke, which seemed a symbolic reminder of the new order. Then my mother phoned to make arrangements for seeing her and Dad at the weekend, which felt like a further nudge. At this age you're no longer a baby to your parents – if you're lucky and your parents are still alive, they may need you more than you need them. You're in the middle of things, in all the most unpleasant ways.

Of course, when you swing it round, there are lots of plusses about looking to a time when your children will need you less and you'll have the opportunity to forge a fantastic new bond with them. Accepting the new order is *not* putting the baby picture back up on the wall in the centre of the sitting room but instead deciding that this is a new era. So I put it in our new box room with a sofa bed, and perhaps I'll put other things from those early mummy days on the shelf in there too – the children's first lock of hair and 'The Teddy Bears' Picnic' curtains. I loved choosing them when I was pregnant so I want to remember that joy, just not have the fact those days have passed shoved in my face every morning.

'Mum, they're seriously not going up in my room,' Darcey said when she saw me lugging the teddy bear curtains into the new house as we moved in. She wanted black ones with silver stars in her new grown-up bedroom. Two of the walls are black and there's a platform bed with a desk underneath and a swivel chair – it's more Bauhaus than nursery and another reminder of the fact that she is soaring away.

Now we're having all kinds of different conversations – the other day she asked me about childbirth and how much it hurts. Why did I not have a C-section, because it would have been much easier, wouldn't it? There's a whole new world of mother-daughter/son interactions coming my way and so much to look forward to, once I've finally let the past go.

My friend Penny emailed me with some titles of books she thought might help with getting a perspective on all of this. Among her recommendations are the writings of Christiane Northrup, an American gynaecologist, obstetrician and women's wellness guru, who has a really positive theory about the menopause and what it means for women. In *Goddesses Never Age* and *The Wisdom of Menopause*, Dr Northrup says that, like adolescence, menopause is a complete rewiring of the brain and nervous system. It's a time of transformation – for the better – when our gaze naturally shifts from the domestic to the wider world, as we deal with the empty nest and fewer demands at home.

OK, perhaps this is Nature's plan.

Dr Northrup says that the veil of reproduction lifts to reveal all the things you didn't do because you were too busy doing things for other people. All those sublimated desires. The times you said, 'I must get round to doing that again,' without ever finding time to do it more than once or twice during the childrearing decades. Suddenly, you're free. Creativity, vocation and self-identity come to the fore again, as they did when you were first striking out. It's crucial to seize this opportunity and nurture your talents and desires.

Research in the psychology department at Manchester University backs up this view. It found that many people experience a creative surge after they are fifty, especially if their responsibilities start to diminish. To name but a few: Anna Sewell wrote her only novel, *Black Beauty*, during her fifties; Laura Ingalls Wilder wrote *Little House on the Prairie* at sixty-four; Antonio Carluccio opened the first branch of his restaurant chain, Carluccio's, at fifty-four; Jack Cover, a World War II test pilot, invented the Taser gun at fifty; Richard Adams published his first novel, *Watership Down*, at fifty-two; the inventor, Walter Hunt, designed the safety pin when he was fifty-three.

There's so much about Dr Northrup's approach that is interesting, because it turns menopausal woe-is-me thinking on its head and says: embrace this! Listen to what your body is telling you and you'll be able to live a fuller life than you did before. Instead of fighting the menopause, work with it, recognise what it's doing and where it's taking you, and allow yourself to be transformed.

Like Helen Duggan, she refuses to buy into the negativity. On the contrary, she says that perimenopause is the beginning of rising into full Goddesshood (I love that!). Menopause makes you wise, gives you courage and renews your fire. Don't mourn menstruation – no longer having periods means that you're 'retaining your sacred Goddess blood and you stop leaking energy'. In fact, you get a massive injection of energy, for better or for worse. 'Life force is sexy,' she says, adding that menopause can be a really sensual time. She's even written a 'playbook' guide to sex as a mature woman.

Two days after I started reading Dr Northrup's theories, my Australian friend Kathy sent me a card that read: 'I'm all out of oestrogen and I've got a GUN.' It made me laugh, but it was a bit frightening too. A lot of people talk about feeling brittle and irritated during the menopausal years; some women describe experiencing utter rage. They feel like Jekyll and Hyde, like unpredictable volcanoes.

As someone who hates confrontation, I don't like the idea of ever erupting like that. I wonder: are menopausal symptoms a midlife woman's equivalent of teenage spots, puppy fat and moodiness? In puberty, life is all racing hearts and heavy petting. Fast-forward thirty-five years and it's palpitations and heavy sweating. Menopause strikes me as a frightening medical experience

– in the way that puberty is – but without the promise of newness that comes after puberty. After all, puberty is an exciting time, even though it's hard to manage.

Dr Northrup argues that the menopause promises, if not newness, then renewal. It's true that the side effects of the hormonal shifts can be extreme, but they each have an important purpose. They are the labour pains of transformation and rebirth. If you feel rage, for instance, you have to ask yourself, what's making me cross here? And take responsibility for it. Yes, it's your hormones – and there are remedies for combating the symptoms – but there's also something triggering your response that you have to face. She warns that if you suppress it, you risk getting ill or depressed, because your anger is telling you that you have to change your life in some way. You need turbulence to break out of the fishbowl. Without it, you'll carry on endlessly swimming around in a circle.

Her books and online talks and interviews offer advice on: hormone therapies; breast, heart and bone health; keeping your weight down; sorting out your finances; dealing with emotional issues; cosmetic surgery, and sex. But it's the central message of her writing that I find so appealing. There are so many ways to make the menopausal years more satisfying then ever, she says. Take control of your life, get proactive about preventing illness and tap into your female spiritual energy.

Her approach corresponds to my general feeling that this is the time of life to put your house in order – and the menopause is the physical side of that, if you're a woman. You can't just carry on doing what you've always done, because you're going through a massive physiological change. Whether or not you're experiencing dramatic symptoms or not, it's time to get as fit, gorgeous, fabulous and positive as you can – to be more *you* than you've ever been before.

CHAPTER 9

Sex and Swinging from the Chandeliers?

There was something different about my French friend Sylvie, the last time I bumped into her. 'How's life?' I asked, expecting a blast of her usual 'My-husband-is-driving-me-crazy-why-did-I-marry-him?' rant. Instead she said, 'Great!' and flashed me a smile straight out of one of those French films where the bored wife starts having a passionate affair with a young Gérard Depardieu, who happens to be living next door.

'What's changed?' I asked, intrigued.

She pouted. 'I gave my husband an ultimatum,' she said. 'Watch less football. Help more with the children. And do the two-week challenge with me.' She paused and gave me a piercing look. Bemused, I asked her what she meant.

'To complete the two-week challenge, you must have sex once a day for fourteen days,' she explained. 'It can be over in seconds or last an hour, it can be in the bedroom or the kitchen, but it must be every single day.'

I resisted the urge to scream, 'Too much information!' and batted away somewhat disturbing images of Sylvie and her husband furiously doing it all over their house.

'Why?' I ventured. 'If it's not a stupid question.'

She shrugged. 'A friend in Paris said it transformed her sex life. I wanted to try it.'

'And how did it go?' I asked.

'Fantastic!' she said, smiling that radiant smile again. She had basically been having an affair with her own husband; her skin was glowing, she had a spring in her step and looked ten years younger. 'You should try it.'

'Babe, I'd love to, but I just haven't got the time,' I said.

It was true. Between work and the kids and having just moved house, everything was in total chaos. It was hard enough finding time to have a conversation with Derek that wasn't about the kids' homework or who was picking who up from where, let alone anything more.

'You have to make the time,' she said. 'That's the point.'

I had sex on my mind for days after I saw her – that beaming, Cheshire Cat grin was hard to erase. She was obviously chuffed to bits about getting on better with her husband, but it was something else too, almost as though there had been a physical change in her. What is it about lovemaking that makes you look and feel better? Millions have been spent on decades of research; I decided to look into the findings. Some of it I already knew – some I absolutely didn't.

Are you ready for this?

A study in Israel showed that women who had two orgasms a week were almost a third less likely to have heart disease. Another study at Queen's University in Belfast found that having sex three times a week could slash your heart attack and stroke risk. Sexual arousal increases your heartbeats per minute, reaching a peak at orgasm, meaning it's good exercise for your heart. Regular sex can ward off heart attacks and stroke, two of the leading causes of deaths in the UK. It lowers blood pressure and stress levels, which we all need to do, and a study in Pennsylvania suggested that it might help strengthen your immune defences and boost levels of immunoglobulins. It is a super-healthy activity.

There's more. Sex ramps up your levels of the natural steroid DHEA, also known as the 'anti-ageing hormone', and increases oestrogen levels, making it a useful antidote to the menopausal slide and osteoporosis. It's a great way for women to exercise their pelvic floor muscles and avoid incontinence. It improves self-esteem, makes you feel better about your body and releases feel-good hormones like serotonin and oxytocin to improve your mood and help you sleep better. And people who have regular sex report feeling healthier. They feel better about themselves, which could also be attributed to the intimacy that lovemaking generates.

So there is every reason to keep it going as you get older, aside from the sheer, spontaneous thrill of it. Sex is *good* for you. Especially as there's now evidence that it improves your cognitive function and appears to ward off dementia, another of the great dreads of later life.

Dementia? Really?

In a study of nearly 7,000 people aged between fifty and eighty-nine, researchers at Coventry University found that the people who were sexually active performed better in mental tests than those who weren't. Women were 14 per cent better in word tests and 2 per cent better in number puzzles and there was an even more marked difference in men (23 per cent and 3 per cent higher scores respectively in men who were sexually active), suggesting that the release of dopamine and oxytocin during sex could be linked to improved memory performance. (Dopamine is a neurotransmitter that helps control the brain's reward and pleasure centres, and oxytocin is a hormone that connects areas of the brain and links them to the brain's reward system.)

So, doctors say it's good for us on lots of levels. Better keep doing it.

The trouble is that, unlike other stuff doctors bang on about, including regular exercise and your five a day, sex isn't just a physical thing, especially when we hit midlife. It's likely to be bound up with all sorts of emotional tangles that our lives and experiences have woven for us over the years.

In a long-term relationship, it can be the source of rows with our partners. If we don't feel as desired as we used to, it can be just another reason to feel that ageing is making us unattractive. It's a tool in power games, and another way we can be made to feel put upon when we're already feeling overstretched and undervalued. For people who are single and trying to find a new partner, it can be scary and yet another thing to be insecure about. Add to that a decline in health and a potentially fading libido after the menopause and it's no wonder that so many people, as they get older, settle for letting sex slide away in favour of a long walk and a good book.

I am not sure being told it's 'good for you' helps either. Don't we want our sex lives (when we get round to having them) to be wild, carefree, naughty and romantic? Turning sex into a plate of curly kale is, well, so *un*sexy.

But let's not panic. Sex isn't the be-all and end-all, as we midlifers know so well. Companionship, trust, support in raising a family and caring for elderly relatives can make us adore our partners much more than any special antics in the bedroom.

If sex is not for you, don't despair. Let's take another look at the evidence in its favour. The increase in your heartbeat during orgasm is often merely the equivalent of walking upstairs, so you could cycle, swim or dance instead. Meditation, fruit, vegetables and exercise can lower your blood pressure; getting a pet can relieve stress and loneliness; and one of my best mates does her pelvic floor exercises in the car while she's waiting for the lights to change. (Or you could get a pelvic toner. The French swear by them and they seem to get most things right.) Exercise, generally, is good for the brain, skin and immune system; calcium tablets strengthen your bones and may ward off osteoporosis. So you can tick all the boxes in other ways. It's just that sex rather handily rolls most of the benefits into one recreational act, regularly repeated.

Either way, if you've never enjoyed sex and you're in your midlife, perhaps you owe it to yourself to explore it. Because otherwise you'll never know, will you? At fifty, your sex life expectancy is at least fifteen years. Thirty per cent of people aged sixty-five to seventy-four still enjoy sex at least once a week. It'll save you a fortune in vitamins and other health remedies. So go for it, if you possibly can.

It's rather handy that someone has written a guide called *Kamasutra Sex Positions for the Over Fifties*. And how about, *Happy Vaginas for the Over Forties* by Claire Preston, with the self-explanatory subtitle: *How to Resuscitate Your Ageing Asset and Protect Her from Menopausal Meltdown*! The information is out there. You just have to grab it.

My friend Margery, who works as a marriage guidance counsellor, says that when the couples she sees have a problem with their sex life, it's rarely just about the physical act itself. So why do the rows boil down to sex? 'Because neither side is able to tackle the real issues, either because they can't quite work out what they really are or because they are too scared to try,' she says.

One of the main reasons marriages go awry, Margery says, is a breakdown in communication. And the risk of this can be even higher in midlife, because for the first few years there is so much to carry couples forward in a joint purpose. The thrill of meeting, getting married, setting up home, maybe having children and raising them, surges us forward. Then as the newness wears off, at each stage the frustrations set in. Frustrations at work, cute toddlers turning into challenging teenagers, money worries, perhaps the demands of parents and older loved ones, less time for fun, for each other and ourselves.

Also couples' roles change – suddenly one might be made redundant and the other starts earning money. She has new power, money, new friends and challenges; he feels lost. Unfortunately, human nature may get in the way and he'll attack her for his own inadequacies. She will leave. They may well both regret it.

I'm friends with a couple who have always been seen as 'the gorgeous one' (her) and 'the clever one' (him). When she got older and began to show signs of ageing, in a panic she started pushing him away. Since he had always thought she was too gorgeous for him, this totally played into his insecurities. He ended up working harder, trying to prove himself to her and live up to what he imagined were her expectations. Meanwhile, she felt more and more isolated. Finally, he had an affair – with someone older! – and she was devastated.

They discussed their predicament in therapy. 'Surely you realised I didn't love you just for your looks. Do you think I'm that shallow?' he asked.

'I wasn't sure there was anything else to love,' she said. 'What do I have to offer other than being pretty?'

'But you have never tried!' he said. 'All you ever wanted was to float around while I was the provider. You can't blame me for seeing you as an ornament – you saw yourself as an ornament.'

Actually he'd *never* seen her as an ornament – it was her kindness and sense of fun that he really loved. But the pressure of endless providing had exhausted him and he wanted time off to do stupid, fun things. They had boxed themselves into roles that neither were that happy with, and each was blaming the other, when they actually needed to take stock and responsibility for the positions they had taken. Fortunately, they worked it through. She started a part-time job, he worked less and spent more time with their children, and they tried to find activities that they enjoyed together.

'Affairs are common,' says Margery, 'but they are rarely about the person you are having the affair with. They happen when people feel that their life is stuck in some way. If you are fed up with your job, under pressure, or feel old and less dynamic, and someone comes along who takes an interest in you and makes you feel dynamic again, there's a chance you may have an affair. If that person is younger, even better, because suddenly you feel younger too. You feel as if you have a chance to do things all over again, and this time do them differently and better. But actually, if you don't sort out what you really want, you will only get to the same place with the next person. First, I would advise trying to instigate the changes you need in a way that means that your current partner doesn't feel lost or pushed away. Remember, they are dealing with their own issues too,' she says.

Of course some relationships aren't meant to be. They can't and maybe shouldn't be saved. But I believe it's worth taking time to work out what you want before you leave. You will have to sort out your baggage one day and trying to work it out with your current partner is a good place to start. You may be surprised at the impressions they have of you and the miscommunications that have become fact. At the very least, it will help you have a better relationship next time around, or give you confidence to build the life that you want, even if it's on your own.

Sometimes you feel unhappy because of your expectations of what constitutes a good relationship. These may be based on how your parents were, or how you see your friends' relationships. But other people's relationships are often very different from the outside looking in, than they are when you are in them. What you are envying might be the front they are putting on to keep up appearances, even though it isn't actually working for them.

I know you have to work on relationships and therapy can help. It definitely helped me make sense of things when my first marriage ended after just a few months. We had seemed like the perfect couple and everyone said he adored me, so it was a horrific shock for me and my friends and family when it didn't work out. 'You are his perfect woman,' people would say. But

I suspect that was the trouble. I had tried hard to be his perfect woman and that was what he had fallen in love with – rather than me.

It was a relationship founded on a total lack of honesty. I don't mean that I lied or hid some ghastly secret. No, I was just so desperate to please that I thought less about what I wanted than about making him happy. For the two years that we lived together before we were married, I was content to go with the flow – and I think it's quite hard to be in love with someone who says, 'Yeah! Whatever! As long as we're all happy.' It means that the other person doesn't ever really get to know you, because you're just drifting along.

If he said he wanted to go on a canal boat for the day, for instance, I was genuinely happy to go on a canal boat. I didn't mind at all – it was a lovely adventure. The problem with just going along with things is that the other person gets into the habit of doing exactly what they want every time. If you don't say, 'Actually, it's a bit cold to go on a canal boat today,' they assume you want to go. You then get into the position where it becomes a really big deal if you say, 'I don't want to do this.'

'WTF? But you always want to ...'

So you don't say it.

When he left, I did the usual and spent many days crying and wailing, drinking wine and singing 'All By Myself', Bridget Jones-style, and asking my friends, my brother Matthew and the rest of my family, 'Why?' Until eventually they could take no more and sent me to a therapist.

The first few sessions were just more of the same – crying and sobbing and feeling like I had let everyone down, not least my family, who had put on a huge wedding. Then, over time, the therapist helped me start to see a pattern. And (of course!) it had all begun in my childhood.

My parents are extraordinary, wonderfully kind and brilliantly clever people, and it is one of the great blessings of my life that I have them. My mum is uber-glamorous and sharp as a whip, but also has a remarkable empathy with people, which definitely worked in my favour as I was growing up – but also, I think, in a way she hadn't intended, it worked against me.

Mum had a way of empowering us by helping us to empathise with others. So I would come home from school and say, 'Mandy has been really horrible to me.'

'What did Mandy say?' she'd ask, then when I told her she'd continue, 'You know, the thing about Mandy is that she is going through a tough time right now. So when she's mean, it's not really about you, it's about her.'

It was fantastic that she taught me to see things from the other person's point of view. As a result, I'm probably quite good at my job covering news events and interviewing people in all sorts of situations, because I can always see the other side of the story. What it didn't do was give me permission to feel cross.

I've only noticed it since seeing how different Derek is with our children. When Billy comes home from school and says, 'David was mean to me today,' Derek will ask, 'What did he say?' and when Billy tells him, Derek says, 'That must have made you feel really cross and I don't blame you, because it's very hurtful.'

Instantly, permission to be upset.

Without realising it, Mum took away that permission. Therefore, all the responsibility for making things work was on me – and I spent a good part of my childhood squishing my anger.

Coupled with that, both my parents are great believers at sticking at things and not giving up just because the going gets tough. When I started taking piano lessons, I found them hard. 'Keep going, it will get easier,' they said. So I did and it did.

Don't get me wrong, I am not blaming them for anything. There is so much they did give me and, now that I am a parent myself, I have learnt that whatever you do or say, however well intended, has an impact on your children and you can't always control how their minds will interpret your actions. After all, my mum and dad's advice was perfectly reasonable – these were laudable things to teach your child and I fully hope to teach them to my children too. And they were only showing me what worked for them. Theirs is a wonderfully happy, fifty-year-long marriage. I can honestly say that, throughout my entire childhood, I never heard them row, except possibly once on a caravan holiday in Wales when my mum read the map wrongly and sent us down a blind alley – and even that was a minor disagreement by most people's standards!

It's just that somehow in my childhood brain I got this all twisted and when I grew up and boys came into focus, I seemed to think it was my job to be perfect for them. I constantly hoped that first dates would lead to second dates, never questioning whether *I* actually wanted to see them again. It was more as if I were at an interview and wanted to be approved for the next stage.

Even when I did speak up, life seemed to teach me that I shouldn't. I started seeing my first serious boyfriend, Andy, at college. We were together for four years and I thought we were going to get married. Our paths diverged but we stuck it out – he wanted to stay in Bath and work, I moved back home to pay off debts and started volunteering at a radio station most weekends, as I was keen to be a journalist.

Then I got a job at the radio station, which meant I couldn't go and see Andy as often. He, understandably, got fed up and began blaming my job. Eventually he dumped me and went out with someone else, which left me feeling devastated. I immediately took it as a lesson that I couldn't have both love and a career, and started trying to win him back, running myself ragged in the process, rather than just accepting that we had outgrown each other, as people in college relationships often do.

From then on, I was increasingly keen to please in relationships – and kept getting dumped. And every time I was dumped, I took it as proof that I was completely and totally unloveable.

What happens then is that you don't pause to take stock during a relationship and you get further and further from real intimacy the more you feel the person slipping away. For some reason, whenever I felt a relationship tailing off, I always assumed I had done something wrong. I couldn't see it as a normal part of learning about love, romance and what worked for me, because I was desperate for it not to end.

So you end up people pleasing to the point where it must be exhausting for the other person – and then you find yourself in a place where you can't even remember why you are there, and they don't know you anyway.

They leave you because you are not a real person any more, just somebody who is desperate to please them. And who wants that as company? It's a stunted personality.

And I was always devastated and overwhelmed by a sense of loss and rejection, even if I didn't like them very much by the end.

Then I met my first husband, who proposed within a month. I was so glad and flattered and determined to make it work that I let my friends and interests fall away – until I found myself alone on the floor of our new married home, the confetti barely out of my hair, wondering where it all went wrong.

Thanks to the amazing support of my brother and the rest of my family and fantastic friends, I climbed back. And things were suddenly different. Because everything I'd done before hadn't worked, all the rules were broken and all the bets were off. I felt weirdly liberated and started going out with people I would never have dreamt of seeing before. Crazy artists, a wild actor and a musician ten years younger than me, who is the kindest, most life-enhancing man I have ever known. It couldn't work out long term because he wanted to go on tour (and is now very successful) and I (by then thirty-six) wanted to settle down and have kids. But for once I didn't blame myself (or him) nor did I struggle to make it work, but finished it (yes, me) – the one and only time I ever have.

Then I ran slap bang into my husband, the loud, larger than life, never-going-to-let-me-get-away-with-anything-other-than-total-honesty Derek.

Obviously it's not perfect. He drives me totally crackers, but at least I know that he wants to be really and properly close to me, and treasures our little family as much as I do.

I don't have regrets about my past relationships, but I realise that I wouldn't have had the heartache if I had been true to myself. I wouldn't have desperately tried to please men who I didn't really want. I'm not asking for sympathy; I know many people have had much rougher love lives in much tougher circumstances. I am sharing this because I believe that sorting out my past helped me to have a better marriage the second time round.

Now it seems to me that, as in so many areas of our lives, getting our sex life and loving relationships right in middle age is all about sorting out the stuff that has built up over the first half of our lives, to make sure the next few decades can be as good as possible.

Having said that, mine and Derek's shared passion for family life means that we get much less time for actual passion than we would like. Which brings me back to my French friend, Sylvie.

I mentioned the two-week challenge to Derek. 'You mean, sex every two weeks?' he said nervously.

I think he might have been having flashbacks to the last time we had sex in a committed way, when we were doing our best to have our second baby. Sex when you're trying to conceive can be awful, because you're always having to do it at the 'optimum' moment, as dictated by pee sticks, hormone levels, cycle charts and clocks.

One of my friends told me that while he and his wife were in a frenzy of timetabling their lovemaking, his third child was conceived at 3 a.m. before he got on the Eurostar to Paris to report on a news story.

'How was it?' I asked.

'Terrible. Who has sex at 3 a.m. while waiting for a taxi?'

It's a story that may resonate if you tried to conceive in your late thirties or early forties. As another mate said, 'I now almost vomit at the smell of a Jo Malone candle, because I used to come in the door, so glad to be home and looking forward to flopping on to the sofa and watching TV, and then I'd get this waft of lime and ginger and think, oh no, she wants to have sex!'

Even if you do get past that, however much you adore your partner, it still isn't easy to find time. How do you stop your relationship becoming something that only exists as the business of running a family?

'Begin with your bedroom. Make it a sanctuary. No phones or tablets next to the bed,' says Margery. 'When you close your bedroom door, your attitude should be, "Thank God that's over. Now, come here, you, let's have a cuddle." It should always be that way.'

'But my phone is one of my alarms, for goodness sake!' I tell her. 'And at the end of the day I just fall into bed feeling beyond relieved that I can go to sleep! And if the sheets are clean, all I'm thinking about is how amazing it feels to have clean sheets!'

'Oh well,' she says, shaking her head sadly.

All right, I'll get an old-fashioned alarm clock and think about how I could turn our bedroom into more of a boudoir. What else?

'Candlelight,' she says, still seemingly unconvinced. 'You both look a hundred times better and so does your bedroom.'

'And always, always wear matching underwear,' says Sylvie in her sternest voice. 'We Parisians wear Princesse tam.tam.'

Really? I think Derek would be confused if it was anything other than big pants! Fine, matching underwear. I'm happy to pick up any crumb of advice a French woman drops, because the French keep coming out in surveys as not being worried that they will lose their attractiveness. They seem to have an innate sexual confidence, which I would like a bit of, please.

'Sex toys could be fun, I've heard,' giggles my bubbly mate, Julia.

'Which ones?' I ask.

Julia lists some of the products available. Electric feather teasers, waterproof remote control vibrators (so you don't have to hold it), vibrating finger pads, something called a fleshlight (a vibrating torch, but I think it's just for men) and musical condoms. It seems that things have moved on from *Sex and the City* – although the rabbit vibrator is still wildly popular. I quite like the sound of sex furniture. A contoured lounger or chaise lounge for making love at just the right angle? They're prohibitively expensive at the moment, but here's hoping IKEA will do a line soon.

'Steve and I do sex date nights,' my friend Fran told me. 'They're the same as date nights, but we go to bed with chocolate truffles and a bottle of champagne instead.'

'Wait, that feels like a bit too much pressure,' I say.

'It doesn't take away the romance, because you're already arranging stuff all the time – nights out to the cinema and going out to dinner. It's just another arrangement, only more fun.'

'But what if nothing happened after all that build-up?'

'If you end up not having sex and just chatting, it doesn't matter either,' she says. 'Don't let it make you feel stressed! It's about blocking out time that doesn't feel pressured.'

Well, I suppose we could just play stupid drinking games and giggle like lunatics instead. 'But the moment I get into bed past nine o'clock, I want to go to sleep!' I wail.

'Schedule an afternoon off, then,' says Fran.

It's a brilliant idea and reminds me of a revelation I had when I was a sleep-deprived new mum and desperate to have a rest. 'Book a babysitter!' my friend Clare Lafferty said.

'But I don't want to go out, I want to sleep.'

'Well, why not book a babysitter to sleep?'

'Can I do that?'

'Of course you can. You book someone to come round for three hours – in the middle of the day, if it's easier – while you go to bed.'

The problem was, I felt guilty. Unless I was doing something specific, like cleaning, working or trying to be nice to my husband, I didn't feel justified in having a babysitter. I felt I ought to be with my child, not sleeping. But actually she was right. Sleep was crucial to being a happy mum and partner, and I guess the same can be said of sex, especially now I know how good it is for you.

Derek has no such compunction, so if we're going out for dinner at eight, he will sometimes arrange for the babysitter to come early so that we can have some time alone. It's not so easy now that the children are of an age when they come into the bedroom complaining that the iPad battery is flat, but it's still worth a try.

Better keep doing it. Although I can't help thinking, what if Derek would rather be in bed with a younger, fresher, more fertile woman?

'Stop it,' he says. 'I just want to be with you.'

If, like me, you've always worried about being fanciable, it makes sense to face up to your demons and conquer them in midlife, in the process becoming empowered.

OK, I thought, let's give Sylvie's plan a try.

Derek sat down with a spreadsheet, our diaries and multi-coloured pens – ooh, the romance! He did the same when I was about to start on *Strictly Come Dancing* – Darcey was only fourteen months old and I was working full time at *GMTV*, so he laid out the week with time coloured in for her (purple), time for work (orange) and time for dancing (green). Every section of the day was perfectly labelled, until he realised there was no colour and no time for him! This time, though, he made sure that he had his own slot every day (red).

Day One went well. It was rather fun, actually. Day Two was not so good, when a nightmare about Harry Potter's fight with Voldemort brought our seven-year-old down into our bed. On Day Three, we had a whole blissful hour to ourselves. On Day Four, Derek suddenly had an extra meeting scheduled in and so we were seriously squeezed for time. On Day Five, I discovered I like tickling. On Day Six, I discovered he didn't.

On Day Seven, I bought a new set of underwear, thinking it would come as a nice surprise. But it wasn't as easy to get off as get on and the bra clasp got caught in my hair. 'Babe, I'm so sorry to ruin the moment, but I need the light on so I can see how to untangle this ...' It quickly turned into a farce, but we laughed our socks off, which was great.

I found I was really enjoying myself. It was an adventure. Even planning it and trying to make it work seemed to make us giggle. Then disaster struck, on Day Eight. Derek had taken the kids to the park while I soaked in a long bath. Running to pick up Billy, he slipped on some leaves and smashed his ankle. Four hours later, he emerged from A&E with four broken foot bones, a full leg of plaster, a wheelchair and instructions 'not to put any pressure on the foot at all, possibly for as long as three months'. Never mind swinging from the chandeliers, just standing under a chandelier was going to be impossible.

But, as we had carved out the time, we used it. I 'cared' for him – something I rarely get a chance to do in our busy lives – and during those hours we had earmarked for romance, I chatted to him and laughed with him to try and distract him from the pain. It was a wonderful time that brought us closer together, which I guess is what Sylvie's experiment is all about. I might not have ended up with her Cheshire Cat-style grin, but I do have a romantic weekend in Rome in three months' time to look forward to, which Derek has booked to thank me for looking after him.

And he says he has checked: there is a chandelier.

CHAPTER 10

Money, Money, Money

Now, this is the one area where I'm sure you're going to think I have no worries. As Danny Baker once said, anyone who works in TV has effectively won the Lottery – because TV presenters are really well paid and live an incredible lifestyle. Thanks to my job in TV, I've been to every continent in the world, apart from South America. I get to go to all the latest shows, often for free, and to the movies as part of my job. I'm invited to fantastic parties. I get a ready-made social life out of it.

The downside is that it only goes with the job. There is no work pension – you're not staff – and you're anxious all the time that at any minute you could be replaced. This is not a random, crazy anxiety like being scared of snakes on a plane. It is a fact, based on evidence, that it is unusual for someone to have been doing what I've been doing for so long.

At the moment, I'm lucky enough to have a job in TV and a job in radio. So by most people's standards, I'm Richard Branson. Only, it's all a bit of an illusion. I'm one of those people who appears to inhabit a glittering world, but while I am definitely wealthy compared to many, the reality, alas, doesn't match the fantasy. Our car is ten years old. Like so many people I've not paid as much into my private pension as I should have. We still have a mortgage on our house. And, let's face it, I'm unlikely to carry on earning what I earn now until the new retirement age – how many 65-year-olds do you see on TV?

There is always talk of an age prejudice in television, particularly regarding women. When I first joined *GMTV*, my boss at the time, the legendary and brilliantly clever Peter McHugh, said, 'Are you enjoying it?'

'I'm loving it!' I told him.

'Do you feel you're well paid?'

'Yes, definitely,' I said. (Probably not the best negotiating tactic, but there you go.)

'Good,' he said. 'A career in television should always be enjoyable and hopefully well paid, because the one thing you can be sure of is that it will be short. Not that I am saying it *should* be short – it shouldn't. That is simply what I have observed over the years.'

'Hmm.' I understood, but I didn't care. I had no responsibilities. I thought, I might not even last until the end of the year, but I'll grab it while it lasts, because it's great.

Things are very different now that the world feels less like my oyster. Some days I look around and all I can see is a small prawn. A prawn with an old car, a mortgage and an inadequate pension.

In reality, the assumption about age prejudice in TV is not true of my experience in breakfast TV, where numerous bosses have made it clear age has never been a factor in their decisions. Indeed, in breakfast TV, they do employ women who are older than the presenters in other areas of TV. Lorraine Kelly is in her fifties, Susanna Reid is forty-six, Charlotte Hawkins is forty-one and Ranvir Singh is thirty-nine They're not old, but they're not twenty-year-olds either, as might be the norm in other branches of TV. We've seen a big change in the last decade and I sometimes think this age fear is purely about the number. It isn't real.

What I think probably is real – what people face in a lot of jobs – is that as you get older and take on more responsibility in your personal life, you worry you will be perceived as less 'useful' as an employee. For me, that means that if the editor rings on a Sunday, albeit to do something amazing, like fly to New York to interview Madonna, I'm suddenly thinking, wait, I've got my parents coming to tea! What about the children's school projects? It's a much harder choice for me now;

I don't want to – and can't – just jump on a plane and disappear at a moment's notice as much as I did when I was single and childless. So you naturally become less flexible and fear bosses might see you as less useful.

Also, you can't stay up all night in an edit and work the next day all the time, because it would be too exhausting and unfair on your family. So even though I know that I'm incredibly lucky still to have my job, I'm aware that things could change at any time. After all, people are always asking me, 'How have you survived?'

'I think it's because I'm cheap,' I usually respond. 'I suspect the producers take a look at me and think, well she may not be the best, but for the money she's as good as we're going to get!'

It's a joke, but it's probably not a million miles from the truth – and the anxiety is always there. How to address it? And how can I shore myself up against financial ruin when I inevitably get the sack?

I was in urgent need of some sensible advice and so I turned to my friend, Martin Lewis, the founder and creator of MoneySavingExpert.com. 'Help!' I said. 'I'm going to be fifty soon. What should I do?'

Let's just say that he wasn't brimming with good news.

'There are no hard or fast rules, because everyone is different,' he told me. 'If you have a high income and no savings, then obviously you are better off than someone who has a low income and no savings. But nothing is guaranteed. The first thing to do is a reality check.'

'Look at the maths', he says. 'Our typical life expectancy is eighty-five and most of us will work for about forty to fifty years of that, which means that the work you do for half of your life has to pay for the whole of life. This takes into account the cross-generational subsidy – as you were paid for by your parents, you in turn pay for your children.'

If you're fifty and have nothing, or very little, you've got fifteen years of working life left to pay for the remaining thirty-five years that you can expect to be alive. *Gulp.* However, getting work is more difficult when you are in the final third of your working life, even though it is estimated that a third of the working population will be over fifty by 2020. There's a high level of unemployment in this age bracket, so we'll probably be seeing a lot more people diversifying, switching careers or portfolios working for different employers, in order to spread the risk of earning a stable income. Hopefully, society will catch up with the changing demographic and ageism will be less of an issue than it is for some people right now. Fingers crossed.

My friend who is a dispatch rider is having a midlife financial crisis because he is looking ahead and thinking, I can't actually be on a bike in the cold and wet in ten years' time. Martin Lewis says that for him –

for all of us – it's time to look at things and re-evaluate, to think about changing career, starting something new, retraining and getting a new set of skills, especially if you're working in an area where you can add to your skill set.

Doing a degree is a good option, because the loan is structured in such a way as to make it very affordable. Midlife internships have been a growing phenomenon in the US for some years and they are on the increase in the UK. Internships are often unpaid, but prove invaluable to people wanting to go back to their careers after a long absence, or wanting to switch careers. Women Returners is a good place to start if you are looking at doing this – they're the organisation responsible for introducing and highlighting the idea of the midlife internship to the UK in 2014.

The Open University offers a range of free online courses that can help former professionals who want to return to work in science, technology and engineering. There are also apprenticeships available in a wide range of areas, including business, administration and law. They may not be easy to get, but if you've decided that's what you need, find out how to apply, feel the power in yourself and make it happen.

Martin Lewis has heard lots of stories of people who are retraining to be plumbers. Craftsmanship in some trades may be disappearing, but people will always need to flush! Becoming a counsellor or psychotherapist is a popular second or even third career. In midlife, people often find they're more suited to this kind of role because they have the experience, understanding and empathy they might have lacked when they were younger. There's a growing demand for therapists, too. Other people forge a new career in education and teaching, where there will always be opportunities for those with life experience.

Sometimes, the way to get on is not about learning new skills, but thinking about what you've already got to offer, what you've done and what your passion is. You may not have qualifications, but what you do have is experience, so perhaps you bring a lot to your job without realising it. Be aware that you may have something to offer above and beyond your job remit. For instance, if you've been working on the shop floor of a supermarket for so long that you see all the pitfalls and mistakes that are being made, you might have a future in management. Rather than thinking, 'Oh the bloody boss has done it again!', consider how you could do it better. Send the boss an email. Think about how you would apply your solutions to your own business.

I started my career in radio partly because I thought I needed to have other options rather than just relying on one TV job. It's an area I've been passionate about as a listener for a long time, but obviously I never considered being a music DJ, because they're the cool dudes, as my daughter would say. 'They do wiki-wiki-wah-wah on a couple of decks – and that's not you, Mum!'

So when the opportunity came up to talk to the head of Global Radio, which manages lots of stations including LBC, I assumed it was for some kind of news job. Instead they asked me to work on a new brand they were relaunching, Smooth Radio. 'We'll train you up to be a DJ,' they said. My jaw dropped. Yes, please. But, will I be able to do it ...?

It meant I had to get my head around a whole new skill and new technology, which was really good for me. After a slightly disastrous training – more on which later – I feel I've found my way and hopefully I bring something to the party. I feel incredibly lucky that something I enjoy so much has given me a new set of skills and upped my employment opportunities.

Still, almost any job you have in the media is precarious, so I can't sit back. What else can I do? 'Look for other ways to boost your income,' Martin says. 'Walk around the house and put everything you haven't used in the last year aside. Ask yourself if you will ever use it again. If not, sell it. Other options include taking in a lodger, renting out your parking space, checking for unpaid tax rebates, renting out storage space and claiming old Tesco vouchers. Google "small schemes to boost incomes" for more ideas.'

All this advice is great as long as you're fit and well. But what happens if you become ill or need assistance in daily life when you're older? Martin Lewis says you should think about how you'll feel if your health goes – and start planning. Now is the time to decide whether you're going to rely on the state or aim for private funding for later life care. Ask yourself what your priorities are. Are you happy for your children to help out with your care, or would you prefer others to wash you, dress you and all the rest of it?

Grimness! Do I really have to think about this now?

'Face the worst,' he says. 'Be prepared.'

Think hard about how you'd deal with what he calls the three Ds: divorce, dementia and death. He said that he meets hundreds of women whose husbands have died and they don't know anything about their money. Some of them still have a mortgage and they don't even know how to pay it, or even which financial lender the mortgage is with. They are absolutely up the creek. So it might be a good idea to have a conversation with someone about how you'd manage. Contemplate how you would cope on your own, if you got divorced or were widowed. If one partner is financially dominant, it's a good idea to draw up a financial fact sheet detailing all the important transactions – gas and electric bills, insurance, pension credits and so on – so that the other partner won't be left in the lurch. Have a financial meeting to discuss what will happen in the event of each other dying. It's never going to be easy, but it is necessary.

You have to be aware that one in three people over sixty-five die with dementia. It's a horrible thought, but it has to be faced. In planning for dementia – or stroke, or an accident – Martin Lewis recommends nominating three people to have power of attorney over your financial matters. This doesn't mean giving away your rights to anything, but in the event of something happening to you, people you trust will be able to handle your affairs. Why three people? Well, it may not be good enough to nominate your husband or partner alone, because they could be in a worse state than you are when the time comes. That's why Martin Lewis suggests organising a chain, nominating one and having two reserves. It sounds bleak, but you need to sit down and think about it. His idea is if you put a plan in place to take care of the 'worst' for the future, you can relax and make the most of the now.

If you opt for state care, you may as well spend your savings before the time comes. At the time of going to press, having less than £14,250 in savings, assets or income means that you won't have to contribute anything to state care. If you have more than £23,250, you will be expected to pay your way. Between the two, the local authority will work out a fair amount for your care home fee contributions.

If you haven't got assets or a pension, you need to manage your expectations about retirement. It's worth asking yourself, what would my life be like if I didn't have what I have now? It's not easy to survive on a state pension. It will keep you fed and comes with a free TV licence, but it won't give you the standard of living that most people aspire to. You'll be taken care of, but you won't be able to have holidays in the Bahamas.

If you're used to a good lifestyle and all you can expect is state help, you need to face up to what that means. Deal with how it's going to be and adjust accordingly. It may help you to prepare if you acknowledge that it's a scary and depressing prospect, because part of getting your head straight is conquering what you're scared of. Thinking it through may make it easier to accept.

I wonder now whether I should have listened to my accountant when he advised me to stop paying into my pension pot. 'This is utterly pointless,' he said. 'Unless you put in four times the amount of money you're contributing every month, it is not going to be enough. You need to focus on property!'

Fashions change, even in the financial world. Now everyone is saying that property isn't enough and you need the pension as well, which is frankly infuriating.

Nevertheless, the one big asset that some people have is their house, and at this age they may be coming close to paying off the mortgage (or not, in my case!). Martin Lewis suggests downsizing now while you can, and getting some cash in the bank. 'I know it's the family house and you love it. But won't it be too big for you once the children have left home? Think ahead to a time when the stairs may get too much for you.'

People say, 'The kids have left home, but we won't sell the house yet because we're enjoying the fact that they come back at weekends.'

Martin Lewis says that some of these people get to sixty or seventy and, before they know it, it feels too late to move. Something may happen like one of them developing dementia. Then it feels wrong to move – even if it's horribly impractical and you're in the middle of nowhere – because one of the things I have found that keeps people going during the early stages of dementia is the utter familiarity of where they are.

Sometimes people don't want to move because they've left it too late to make new connections in a new area. That's why planning ahead is so important. If you stay too long and it's too late to move, your only option for generating cash will be equity release – in other words taking out a loan secured against your home to generate a lump sum or steady stream of income, to be repaid at a later date after you've died. That's not such a bad outcome if you're not planning to leave your money to anyone, but it isn't great if you are, because of the vicious compound interest that accumulates on the loan. The more you take out and the earlier you do it, the more expensive it will be. If you do decide to go that route, Martin Lewis suggests going through the Equity Release Council.

Once you have downsized, the older you are, the less risk you want for your money. Saving won't generate income at the current low interest rates, but investment is risk. Be prepared to lose money if you invest in stocks, shares or bonds, and accept that you won't see a radical difference if you save.

God, it's all a bit depressing, isn't it? The horizon is looking rather bleak.

I needed some good news, so I rang my friend Penny Stokes-Hilton, who at fifty upped sticks and moved to Florida, where she runs a business. Penny seems to have it all. She's living in the sunshine, being busy and vibrant, looking great and getting the most out of life. I think I'd like to be where she is.

'Penny,' I said, when we'd finally negotiated the time difference and found a moment when we could both speak. 'You have the life that everyone wants. What everyone wants to know is, how did you do it?'

'Out of absolute desperation and destitution,' she replied.

She wasn't joking. Penny and her husband Ian had already planned ahead, downsized and let go when Ian was suddenly made redundant after being in his job for twenty years. 'We'd bought a funny little bungalow and made it gorgeous,' she says. 'We had security and a pension. There was a comfortable rhythm to our lives. I thought we had life sussed. But I was wrong. You don't have control of anything, really.

'When the company Ian was working for went bust, everything seemed to go with it: the company car, the pension and the easy life. I was fifty at the time,' she said, 'and I'd been working hard to keep my energy and sparkle, but suddenly it was less about feeling happy at fifty than how are we ever going to survive? Who was going to give Ian a job?'

After thirty years in building and construction, her husband was a senior site manager in charge of 200 people, but his experience was overlooked by companies who just wanted cheap, available labour.

'That must have been awful,' I say.

'I felt sick,' she agreed. 'I thought we were done for. How were we going to turn this around? I knew we would have to sell the bungalow and move into somewhere smaller – perhaps even a caravan.'

'So you went to live in Florida?' I asked. 'That's quite a leap.'

'I had always loved America, so I said, "Why don't we go to Florida and get some sunshine?" I felt I could cope living in a tiny space in a warm climate better than I could in rainy England. What I didn't want to do was just sit there feeling powerless thinking, I'm going to end up in a tiny council flat or a caravan before long.

'"OK, let's do something mad," she told Ian. "Let's pack up and go to America for a couple of years. What have we got to lose? If it doesn't work out, we can say it was a bad year and come back knowing we've tried." You can never feel completely bad about trying something, even if it doesn't work.'

Although Penny had no qualifications, she knows how to think on her feet – and she drew on her energy and sparkle to get motivated. Four years ago, she put their house on the market and their life – nine suitcases – in a container in the UK. She and Ian set out for three months, thinking that the worst-case scenario would be that they had to return and accept their fate.

'If for some reason life closes a door on you, don't try to reopen it,' she told me. 'Seek out a door that may be ajar and try that one instead.'

'And?'

'Dreams can come true if you have the courage to believe. I believed that I could live in the sunshine with a swimming pool and I made it happen.'

She and Ian based themselves close to Disneyland and tried to find work cleaning and maintaining the holiday homes in the area. Then they spotted that families that came on holiday often didn't bring their buggies because of luggage restrictions on flights and walking around all those theme parks gets very tiring. So they started a business hiring out prams. At first they had one buggy; now they have sixty. Then this expanded into cots for apartments that didn't cater for tiny babies, and then barbecues for Brits who wanted to make the most of the Florida sunshine. Three cots became 150 cots. Six grills became 120 grills. One little van turned into three huge trucks. It took months of hard grind, eighteen-hour days and dogged determination. They didn't stop for breath for the first year.

Penny explained: '"Hello, we are Penny and Ian from England!" we'd say and turn up at places with a big tray of doughnuts, trying to win favour with the holiday reps, trying to get them to use our services hiring out buggies and grills. They wouldn't say yes straight away, but then one day their own service company would let them down and they would remember that funny little couple from England who brought them doughnuts and ring us up. So the company just grew and grew.'

Penny and Ian started to look around for other opportunities that meant they didn't have to work such long days, so that they could build an easier future.

Penny's passion was, and always has been, houses and property. She had tried to be an estate agent in England but hadn't got beyond a second interview. Now she was determined to try again. Facing down her fear that no one would take her seriously at fifty, she took her real estate exam, failed twice, eventually passed and flew into a career making property sales. 'It felt a bit strange sitting in lessons with twenty-year-olds,' she said. 'But over here people like the fact that you are older.'

I made a mental note about moving to Florida. 'The horizon suddenly looks a lot brighter,' I said.

'Yes, there we were, on skid row, thinking the good life or indeed any kind of life was over – and here we are now!' she said happily. 'Ian is successful; he's gone from working out of the garage to having an office and staff. He could barely turn a computer on when we came here – it was one email a year. Now he's organising the entire company online.'

'Isn't it really hard to get a permit to work in America, though?' I asked.

'It's not as difficult as you think,' she said. 'But you have to achieve a certain turnover, so you can't just coast. You have to prove you're earning a certain amount, there's a yearly assessment to check it and then your visa needs to be renewed by the embassy.'

'Don't you miss your children, your parents?'

'It's funny, isn't it? The children feel they're free to go off and come back when they want, yet Mum isn't allowed to disappear. But they'd left home and were living their own lives for themselves, understandably, and I felt I didn't want to be a burden on them, so we had to make a decision. Our situation in the UK wasn't great and I decided that you can't live life for other people, because you'll turn into a martyr, depressed about life and miserably scared for the future. I thought, my kids are embracing their lives. My parents have had their lives. I need to think about my own life. And anyway Facetime makes the world a smaller place, and we've worked so hard we can help to pay for them to come over to stay with us.

'Look, it's a huge risk, and it still all may go wrong tomorrow, but at least I know I've tried. I have the potential for a retirement in the sunshine. It's a far better outlook than we had five years ago.'

I'm so inspired! Penny solved her problem by upping sticks and reinventing herself, doing things she never dreamt she could do. She started her own business, when she never thought she could. She's a great example of how you can change your life.

After I put the phone down, I sat on the sofa and imagined myself soaking up the sun beside a swimming pool in Florida. With Derek, of course. But then I realised there is no 'of course'. I feel my marriage is very strong but so do many people before fate takes a turn – and besides, maybe he'll become too annoying even for me!

What would happen to me financially if we did go the way of the silver splitters? Would a grey divorce leave me up the creek without a paddle? It isn't going to make me richer – it's far more likely to involve a lifestyle downgrade, and possibly a dramatic one. It's not like getting divorced in your thirties, painful as that might be, when there are all kinds of job and training opportunities ahead of you. Divorce in midlife is often a choice between staying in a soulless marriage or taking the financial hit in the hope that you will find happiness, and not loneliness, on the other side. After years of sharing experiences and memories, do you dare to go it alone?

I've decided that Derek isn't that annoying after all. Which I'll take as a good sign.

If you've got a decent job, you may be able to weather the financial upheaval of divorce quite well – something that would have been more difficult even a generation before ours. Whatever the state of your marriage, it's a good idea to separate your finances, or at least know what there is and where. Other crucial information is whether your name is on any bills or excluded from any savings accounts, and whether you both have up-to-date wills. If you don't already know, you might want to look at whose name the house is in. Think it through and get legal advice.

If you go for a divorce even though it's going to leave you a lot worse off financially, hats off to you. When living with strangers is a better prospect than living with your other half, you obviously feel it's worth getting away. You may have to go back to house sharing, which could potentially be a bit miserable unless you luck out with your housemates, but sometimes there's enough coincidence in people's lives that they are able to move in or buy a house with friends. Facebook is a great place for keeping up with what everyone is doing. If you keep your presence active and work on extending your network, you never know what opportunities might come up, from mates old and new.

So where do I find myself now, apart from wandering round my house wondering if Derek would notice if I sold his whisky collection?

My kind, clever friend, Martin Lewis, has given me plenty of food for thought. I think I'm ready to make a plan.

Remember Penny. Draw on your sparkle, and if it feels right, make that leap.

CHAPTER 11

Popping Your Clogs

'I thought I'd save the best till last,' I told Derek.

'And that is ...?' he asked, looking hopeful.

'Death,' I said.

'Terrific,' he laughed.

I think he meant terrifying.

There are lots of scary things about getting older, but one of the biggest, I guess, is death itself. Especially in midlife, when we suddenly wake up to the fact we may have fewer years left than we have already lived. It certainly frightened me. It increasingly dominated my thoughts, waking me up in the night in cold sweats. I couldn't really understand then why it gripped me so suddenly and so much, but it did. And no amount of jokey comments like, 'Don't think about it, there's nothing you can do anyway', could take the fear away.

So I decided that, if I was going to really be master of myself in midlife – and tackle all the things that scared me about ageing – I had to take on my biggest fear of all and stare it down. And the results were amazing, life-changing even, so please do read on – I promise this chapter isn't as morbid as you might think!

My way, so far, of tackling life's challenges had been essentially to draw on my work skills and approach them like a journalist. First, loads of research – finding out all there was to know about a problem. Then, finding people who had experienced it and asking a million questions to try to find out what they had learnt. But there was a problem with using my journalism for this one because, of course, no one who had died was around to tell the tale. And it was the not knowing that haunted me. How did it feel to die? And not just to be dying, or coping with the final stages of failing health, but the actual moment when life slips away and what lies beyond. How to get my head round that?

Of course, all the major and minor religions have their theories of what happens next, ranging from a heavenly afterlife for the soul, hell, limbo, paradise or reincarnation, but there's no proof – and I wanted facts. It's almost more comforting to think that there isn't anything, that death is a bit like going for a general anaesthetic, something deeper than going to sleep.

'The time to be happy is now,' said Robert G Ingersoll, the nineteenth-century humanist. Meaning, there's probably no afterlife, so stop worrying and enjoy today.

But how? Would I enjoy lunch with my mates if I knew I had root canal surgery at three? At least I know what root canal surgery is, whereas with death, how could I ever really know? And how to live with the not knowing?

'Well, you could start by actually using the word,' said my friend Ranvir Singh, who lost her father when she was only nine, and consequently had to come to terms with death and the impact of it at a very young age. 'You do realise that you've been talking for ten minutes about your fear of death without actually using the word?'

It was true, I did my best to avoid saying it. Even when reporting on the demise of a star or famous name, I would opt for 'passing away', which I'd kid myself sounded gentler, somehow, and less final. In other instances, I preferred using jokey expressions like 'kicking the bucket' or 'popping your clogs', which made it simply sound like another one of my calamitous mishaps, and much more palatable. Then there were the phrases that made death sound like a great adventure – 'jumping on the last rattler' and 'joining the great majority', which was my uncle's favourite euphemism. I loved that one, as it made death sound like something popular and agreeable that you chose to do, and a natural conclusion to life.

It turned out that 2016 was not a year to be a news presenter who was scared of using the word 'death' ... It seemed that every week some beloved icon of my youth was passing away, and we were running tributes and interviewing those who had known and loved them on *Good Morning Britain* and Smooth Radio. With each person who died it seemed to remind me that my days were numbered too. These stars from my youth came with so many memories; of discovering them with teenage friends, listening while I studied for exams, the soundtrack to dates, to new and adventurous nights out with mates. As each one passed I felt the earthquake of mortality and a sadness that those days were gone.

David Bowie – on my wall as a child – seemed to speak for a whole generation. I listened while Annie Lennox, who knew him well, told of how much of a loss he was, and how he had made peace with his own imminent death. Yet, as she spoke, she barely said the word, almost as if he couldn't *be* dead. Instead she focused on what lived on in his music.

I saw Ronnie Corbett with his wife, Anne, what seemed like just weeks before he passed away, still very much full of fun and generous to the end. And I saw Paul Daniels' wife, Debbie McGee, only days after his passing. She was still in shock, but said how much they had laughed and he had found joy, seeing the best in life right to the end.

I wondered how to reach this state that their loved ones spoke of, this calmness. Perhaps it came because they knew the end was near and had a chance to face it with no regrets, no fear, just peace with the circle of life.

It also struck me just how even the people closest to those who are dying, those who were utterly embroiled in it, still avoided using the word death. Maybe it was denial, or it felt too painful to say it. Or maybe it was because even those close to death are too scared to say it out loud, like the witches and wizards in Harry Potter who didn't want to speak Voldemort's name in case it made the evil wizard more real and gave him greater power. I decided I was going to be like Harry Potter when he prevented Hermione and Ron from using the term 'You-know-who' and dared to say 'Voldemort' out loud.

When you think about it, why really should any of us avoid using this word? As my uncle's favourite euphemism for death, 'joining the great majority', illustrates, death has been around since the world began. In fact, to die is to have been alive, as natural as breathing, as the seasons, as life itself. So maybe naming it would help to take its power over me away. Well, it was a start anyway.

Maybe I went a bit too far, dropping it into every conversation at every opportunity. I spoke about plants dying, pets dying and relatives dying. When the milk went off, I wondered aloud whether it had actually died. The sight of the last leaves falling off the trees in our garden made me sigh and wax lyrical about life's seasons – and death, its winter.

Eventually, Derek said, 'Er, I am proud of you for trying to get your head round this, but is there any chance you could drop death, you know, from every conversation in daily life?'

'I have to tackle this,' I said. 'I don't want to go on feeling anxious about it through my fifties and sixties.'

'Well, maybe just dial it down a notch,' he said. 'Because it's a bit of a conversation killer ...'

That's an understatement. We're not very good at dealing with death in the Western world. We're obsessed with improving our health and living longer, but we spend all our time avoiding the inevitable outcome to life. We're very different from the Victorians, who lived on average until their late forties amid heart-breaking levels of mortality, but openly debated death in a way that would seem morbid today. Surrounded by the dying, they dealt with their grief by endlessly talking about it. Needless to say, it was boom time for spiritualists.

Things changed in the twentieth century, perhaps because the staggering fatalities of the two World Wars proved to be too tragic for the communities that bore them, or maybe because the deaths took place on battlegrounds far away, out of sight. People became tight-lipped about death and a taboo grew up around it.

Fast-forward to the twenty-first century and our heads are still in the sand. Millions of people don't write wills, have life insurance or discuss their end of life or funeral wishes with their partners – or anyone else. Seven out of ten people would like to die at home but more than half of us die in hospital, according to the Dying Matters coalition, a charity that works to widen the debate about death, bereavement and end-of-life care. What people fear most about death is pain, suffering, inadequate care and upsetting their loved ones, but they don't do anything to mitigate these things. We want a so-called 'good death', but we won't discuss it.

It makes sense – and the consensus is – that you're more likely to have a good death if you face it head on. And more than that. You are more likely to have a sunnier, happier life, if you tackle the black cloud of death – if you talk about it, do the paperwork, plan where and how you want to die, think about your funeral and deal with unresolved issues with friends or family while you are still able to do so. The author, George Eliot, was perhaps over-egging the pudding when she said, 'I think of death as some delightful journey that I will take when all my tasks are done,' but it's still a good point.

Death will never be a happy topic, but there is help with addressing it if you need it. The late psychiatrist,

Elisabeth Kübler-Ross, who co-founded the hospice movement around the world, wrote a groundbreaking book, *On Death and Dying,* in 1969. Kübler-Ross is perhaps best known for her research into the different stages of grief – denial, anger, bargaining, depression and acceptance – but she also recognised that denial around the subject of death was detrimental to people who were dying. She advocated an honest, compassionate approach to patients and highlighted the importance of listening to and interpreting their needs. Her pioneering work involved using the testimonies of dying people to construct a model for how to care for them. And anyone who has been to a hospice knows that, far from being the sad, fearful places you might imagine them to be, they can be peaceful and even joyful. The tears and sadness come more from the waiting rooms, from the relatives and friends who are losing their loved ones.

Kübler-Ross's influence seems very apparent in The Art of Dying Well website. Set up by the Catholic Church of England and Wales, it aims to help people think about what a good death might mean for them by tackling the subject head on. It shines a light on the different phases, stages and perspectives of death using short animations and films about people who are dying, their loved ones and carers. And as well as giving space to the spiritual meaning of faith and death, it's also a comforting, practical and useful resource if you're facing the death of a loved one, or your own death, and is packed with information, advice, contact numbers and links.

Elisabeth Kübler-Ross says in her writing that faith can be an important element in smoothing the way to a peaceful death. If you genuinely believe in a religious afterlife, you're not going to feel the same conflict and fear around dying as people who feel uncertain about what is waiting for them beyond death. Interestingly, true atheists often die in a similarly untroubled state, she says, because they don't doubt that death is the end and don't worry about what it means. It's the doubters who have the problems. Unfortunately for me, I'm one of them.

My grandparents probably influenced me more than anybody else in this area of my life. My mother's parents were perhaps not totally convinced by organised religion, but were very spiritual all the same. My grandfather felt very connected to nature. He used to take me on long country walks and point out all the signs of the changing seasons and the natural circle of life. He was a six-foot former Rugby Union player, but nature's brutal beauty frequently moved him to tears. I remember one freezing February we spotted a snowdrop pushing up through the snowy ground. The tears flowed as he said to me, 'Just look at that tiny, delicate thing fighting against the elements to survive – that is the power of our life force, Katy.'

At other times he would show me the stars at night and talk of the vastness of the universe and how little we really understood it. We discussed the fourth dimension, time, and he explained it to me by saying that if a two-dimensional man lived in a two-dimensional house, it would be a flat square on the ground. We, living in a three-dimensional world, could happily walk into that square and the two-dimensional man would be terrified, thinking, 'How could they have got in here?' Grandpa wondered with me whether people – or their energy, their 'souls' – could in fact move through time, the fourth dimension, just as easily, but we, stuck in a three-dimensional world, couldn't understand it. 'Time connects us to the people who came before', he would say, going on to talk of his past and his parents and their parents. He explained that their energy moved through him into me and was all around us, in a way we didn't fully understand yet. I loved this idea.

Meanwhile, my Garraway grandparents were more traditionally spiritual. They were devoted churchgoers and belonged to a lovely Church of England church in their village in Berkshire, where Grandpa Garraway was a verger and my grandmother used to play the organ. They were keen for me to go to Sunday School and I enjoyed going to church with them and seeing how much it was part of their lives. The singing was wonderful, and sometimes my granny let me play the organ, because I played the piano.

My grandmother's family ran a brickyard and my great-grandfather's wedding present to his daughter and son-in-law was the bricks to build a house. My grandfather, being a carpenter and builder, constructed a lovely house, and he and my granny moved in there when they got married and lived in it for the rest of their lives. Their involvement in the church gave them a vibrant social life and put them at the very centre of village life. Grandpa and my uncle – who also became a verger – often found themselves assisting at a christening, a wedding and a funeral in the same weekend. They called it 'hatching, matching and dispatching – the circle of life'.

They had some real Dave Allen-style stories about burials, darkly humorous tales of graves getting flooded and how the coffin kept floating up during the burial ceremony and they had to weigh it down with a ladder. It was all that black comedy that surrounds death, which I think probably helps to diminish fears about it. Certainly, my grandparents seemed very calm at the prospect of death. Their faith was a huge part of that, too.

My grandpa Garraway was rejuvenated in old age. I remember him as quite a stern grandfather when I was a little kid. He would come in after a long day at work and there was a big fuss about getting his tea on the table. I suppose he was exhausted; he worked really hard. But when he retired, he became this jolly, free person. Suddenly he had time and took a lot of pleasure in us, his grandkids. He was a great example of old age.

My grandfather Garraway died peacefully in bed when he was ninety-three. He had cycled into the village earlier in the day and later had a meal with my grandmother. Then he said, 'I'm going on up to bed, Connie. I've got indigestion.' Only, it wasn't indigestion, it was the start of a heart attack and that night he died.

I was abroad when he passed away and of course I was very upset when I came back. He was the first person close to me who had died. I went with my brother, Matthew, to the funeral parlour. 'Do you want to see him?' my father asked.

I said yes, almost without processing what that meant. It was a shock seeing his body – the first dead body I'd seen – because he was exactly the same but completely different. Whatever made him Grandpa had gone.

I realised then that there is an energy and a life force that isn't just about the mechanics of the body. It's not just a bundle of cells – and the energy goes somewhere, I'm sure of that. It's not lost around the universe. Energy is always transferred. But I don't know whether you come back as a worm, or you go to a place with angel wings on, or how the energy recycles itself.

While all these thoughts were churning in my head, my producer friend, Vickie, called. 'What are you up to?' she asked breezily.

'Just trying to tackle my fear of death,' I said.

There was only a slight pause before she said, 'You could hedge your bets and have your body cryogenically frozen. I read that it costs around twenty grand. Apparently, Simon Cowell has put his name down for it.'

Well, I wouldn't be surprised at that. If anyone was going to take on death, then surely it would be the god of popular television, Simon Cowell. Although utterly charming and great fun to be around, there's no doubt that Simon Cowell is formidable – just the sort to make the Grim Reaper shiver in his boots.

I remember the first time I interviewed him, just as he launched the first series of *The X Factor.* I had bought a brand-new dress, a bit too tight – I hadn't yet learnt that being comfortable is by far the best way to go when taking on a nerve-racking project. So I was already sweating and squirming when he arrived. The producers were too nervous to do the interview for *GMTV* live, because Simon has a reputation for preferring not to get up early, and often running late. When telling me about his own experiences on *The X Factor,* Dermot O'Leary once joked, 'There are moments when we all mourn the Gary Barlow years. When he was head judge we would always start in the morning, on time.

With Simon Cowell, you are lucky to start recording the *X Factor* auditions before nightfall!'

So there was no way we could risk putting him on the show live, as he would probably turn up sometime during *Jeremy Kyle*! So we met late morning and he arrived, charming and friendly, but I just fell apart. I got up to say hello too quickly and knocked over a mug of tea, narrowly missing his perfectly pressed high-waisted trousers, and stumbled over my 'Hello'.

'Ooh, I don't seem to have the X factor,' I joked. 'I'm not making a very good start at this, am I?'

'No, you're not, Kate – it's really disappointing,' he said with that famous Cowell honesty.

I shrivelled. So I could just imagine the Grim Reaper shrivelling in his presence too – or maybe he'd just turn up too late for their appointment and Death would move on!

Either way, if super-smart Simon Cowell was considering freezing his body, it was worth looking into. Although it did sound like a long shot, especially as it might take a century for medical science to find a way to revive me. And surely way too much could go wrong? I kept flashing on that science fiction movie *Coma*. I decided that I didn't want to wake up in the middle of some kind of floating corpse nightmare.

But when the heartbreaking story broke in late 2016 about the fourteen-year-old with terminal cancer who asked to be cryogenically frozen when she died, I thought again.

We covered the story on *Good Morning Britain* and I interviewed a doctor who works in cryogenics. 'I don't necessarily believe that we will get there in ten, fifty or a hundred years,' he said. 'But believing that there is something after death is vital to making the most of whatever your life is, I think. So, since I don't believe in heaven, I'm going to believe in cryogenics and I will be freezing my body.'

He was very persuasive, but I'm still not sure. Reading about the enormous Timeship building in Texas – which is currently under construction and is being built to withstand bombs and natural disasters – slightly gives me the heebie-jeebies. If all goes according to plan, it will be the world centre of cryopreservation, with space for tens of thousands of frozen bodies, along with human DNA samples, cells, tissues and organs. Yet it could be a literal lifesaver if it's true that our personalities, memories and identities are stored in long-lasting structures within the brain. Yes, it's a long shot, but so far scientists have managed to freeze and defrost a rabbit's brain intact, according to reports. So they're definitely working on it.

But whether you're frozen or not, you still have to die – and that's where my worries lie. How do I get to grips with that?

'There's a vicar in Germany who will let you lie in an open grave to meditate on death,' my old college mate Joe said, who finds the whole subject fairly amusing.

I could do that, or I could go to a weekend workshop where a group of you talks about different aspects of death. What sort of person gives up a weekend to do that? I'd love to know. As the workshop unfolds, would it be insensitive to say things like, 'Let's not flog a dead horse here,' or, 'Can we move on? We've done this subject to death.' I'd worry that I wouldn't be able to resist.

'What about a Buddhist retreat, where you sit and think about death in silence for days on end?' Joe said.

'Me? A silent retreat?'

He guffawed.

One sensible suggestion came from my spiritual and practical friend of twenty-five years, Clare Holt, who recommended seeing a healer who works with terminally ill people to help them come to terms with their own end. That's how I ended up in a room in West London talking about my fear of death with Annie Penny, a trained healer, counsellor and therapist. Annie does a lot of her work with people who are dying – in hospitals, hospices and at their homes – but as she kept on pointing out with alarming optimism, 'We're all dying!' It's something we all have to face, whether or not we've had a diagnosis.

'Healing does not always make people better,' she explained, 'but it helps them with their acceptance of death, which after all is a very natural part of life. It is only society that makes us fear it to the degree that we do.'

I booked myself in for a healing session.

Annie uses techniques that draw upon the parts of the world where death isn't so feared, but instead working towards a good death is actually seen as a positive goal of life. She practises an emotional release technique commonly known as 'tapping', or Emotional Freedom Technique (EFT), and she goes beyond releasing emotions into clearing the chakras, which are the seven centres of spiritual power in the body central to yoga, meditation and Ayurveda. The seven chakras of the body correspond to the body's major nerve centres and organs, and they align the spine from the base to the top of the head. 'Chakra' is a Sanskrit word meaning 'wheel' and the theory is that, to stay healthy and vibrant, it's important to keep the wheels spinning freely.

Blocked chakras may lead to illness or unhappiness, and spiritual healing is about clearing them. In Annie's view, everything is about energy in the body and how we manage it. She believes – and physics seems to support – the idea that death is simply a matter of energy moving. If you look at it this way, it instantly seems less fearful – or at least it does to me.

People who are facing death go through similar stages of grief to the bereaved. There's anger and depression, understandably. There's also denial, which can manifest in pretending they haven't got cancer and not telling anyone, or running around getting second opinions and trying everything going to try and cure it, even though they've been told there's no chance. Healing attempts to help people through those stages to come to a state of acceptance – even happiness – by opening up a spiritual sense. Even if they've never been religious, or they've been anti-religion, they often gain a state of calm because the body wants relief from all the stresses and tensions it has stored up and from the endless tapes that run in our heads.

Annie had a lot of very interesting things to say about midlife too, particularly the menopause, which she views as a surge in energy. She thinks that the people who don't deal very well with it sometimes have unresolved issues. If you're lying awake at night in a boiling hot sweat having a miserable time, with fire coming out of you, something is definitely off-kilter. It may be that menopausal symptoms wake you up and then your troubles don't let you go back to sleep, whereas if you've dealt with your issues, you can tell yourself it's just the menopause, relax and drift off. Our bodies are constantly fluctuating between balance and imbalance, she says. Keeping the chakras clear is an essential part of maintaining the balance.

Part of me thinks this all sounds a bit hippy-dippy, but Annie is very reassuring. She's about my age, seems very down to earth and has the air of a glamorous mum. Her previous career was in business publishing and something of that persona lingers. I like her.

EFT works by stating your greatest fear out loud and tapping meridian points on your body at the same time. Meridian points are regarded as energy hotspots in Traditional Chinese Medicine and tapping them helps to restore the flow of energy. Annie tapped a point on my hand because I hadn't learnt to do it myself yet. She told me to say out loud my greatest fear.

I started off by saying, 'I fear death.'

I had to keep saying it over and over again.

'What about death do you actually fear?' she asked, tapping away.

She had to ask the question several times before I could say, 'I think it's the not knowing.'

Now she had something to work with, she encouraged me to say, 'Even though I have this fear of not knowing what death is, I love and accept myself completely.'

It's the sort of thing that instinctively I want to run a mile from. It sounded like such hippy drivel, and all that 'accept myself' – so Oprah!

All my self-doubting and utter lack of self-confidence surged up to reject it, but I overruled it. Let's give it a go, I thought.

'Do you have an image in your head?' she asked me.

'I think it's the "aloneness" of it,' I said. 'The fact that even if someone is holding your hand, at the moment you actually die you have to pass over on your own, with no one to guide you – not knowing.'

Suddenly I was unable to speak or breathe. My throat was so constricted that it felt as if somebody had their hands around it. I started to cough and struggle for breath.

'Are you having a reaction?' she asked.

'I can't really speak. My throat feels really tight, like I am being strangled,' I croaked.

'This is brilliant!' she declared. 'It's your throat chakra, which controls communication, emotional self-expression and truth.'

It was hilarious that she was so positive about it! I was actually thinking, this is NOT brilliant, I could be choking here and facing my fear of death by actually dying! But I suppose it's one way to cure it...

Annie encouraged me to think of images from my childhood when I might have had this pain in my throat before.

'I've always been susceptible to throat and gland problems,' I gasped.

'Keep breathing,' she said. 'Glandular fever, tonsillitis?'

'All of that. I had tonsillitis continually, and very badly at university, just before finals. And I have had an overactive thyroid and glandular fever since.'

'This is marvellous news! You're obviously someone who stores all your stresses and fears in your throat. Think of a time when you first remember feeling it.'

I was about six or seven when I first started fearing death. It was very soon after my mum had been into hospital to have treatment for her overactive thyroid. In those days, more than forty years ago, it was normal practice to remove a huge chunk of the thyroid. She came home looking like something from Halloween, with clamps on her neck.

While she was away, I was fine. It was all a bit of a novelty. I remember my dad burning the bacon because he couldn't cook, which my brother and I found hilarious. But when Mum came back, I started fearing death in a tangible way for the first time. As for many children, my parents were my whole world. My mum made my childhood full of magic, always inventing fun and fairy stories, even a simple trip to the shops became an adventure. My dad too. He also made me feel constantly safe, still does, guiding me through the challenges of life. I know I am so lucky to have always had them and to still have them with me. My mum's absence for her operation meant I started to wonder what life would be like if they weren't there, and it was terrifying.

I talked to Annie about this while she was furiously tapping my meridians. 'My mother has a story that she tells about this time. We were on a bus and I asked her, "When does time stop passing?"

'Everyone on the bus looked at her as if to say, "Wow, big parental challenge! Let's see how you do on this one."

'My mum gulped. "Well, it doesn't really stop passing, what do you mean?"

'"When does it end? When does it all stop?"'

Mum knew I was thinking about death and dying. Soon afterwards, I went through a very strange period of not being able to sleep and asking lots of questions about death. It ended when we saw a dead hedgehog at the side of the road. Fortunately, it wasn't squished flat and looked rather peaceful. Something clicked in me and my mum says it was as though some of my fears were quietened and questions answered.

As I finished telling Annie this story, I felt an incredible pain in the top of my head, literally as if someone was stabbing it.

'Excellent,' Annie said. 'The energy has moved from your throat to the crown chakra, which is your connection to enlightenment, spirituality and the divine.'

In this sense, she believes, the divine is something other than yourself – a higher or spiritual being, if you like. So, opening up that chakra connects you to your higher self and a higher being. She also said it shows you are letting your anxieties go – giving them up to the 'divine'.

We went on talking. 'Is this really a simple fear of your own death and not knowing?' Annie asked. 'Or has it somehow merged with childhood fears about the loss of your parents and maybe how that will change life for you?'

While Annie went on tapping, I thought about a very specific memory I have of a teacher calling a girl out of our chemistry class to tell her that her dad had had a heart attack and died. I remembered my fear of what this meant, and of how the girl came back to school a week later saying that it was the worst time of her life.

That fear of loss has surged through me at various points in my life as an adult. One moment in particular was around 3 a.m. on a cold Sunday morning. Clare Nasir and I were walking through Hyde Park in shorts and sparkly bras; it was the annual MoonWalk, a twenty-six-mile power-walking marathon in aid of breast cancer, which starts at midnight. Competitors are encouraged to dress up and decorate their bras as crazily as they like – quite a sight for the unsuspecting partygoer staggering home in the early hours to be faced with thousands of women in their underwear pacing the streets of London! We were on mile sixteen, aching all over and really struggling. At one point Clare says she actually heard my blister pop! Thousands of competitors had dispersed ahead of and behind us (mainly ahead!), but in Regent's Park we caught up with a group of girls, all in their custom-made bras. From the back, we could spot their safety-pinned bibs, which showed their race numbers, and an extra piece of paper pinned below, with carefully written words.

'In memory of my mum.'

'I love you, Mum, you're with the angels.'

Clare and I were silent as we walked along, both quietly crying at the thought of their loss.

'But your parents are still alive!' said Annie, still furiously tapping away. 'You have taken their *real* loss and are living an *imagined* version of it even before it has happened.

'Have you had someone close to you suffer loss – and did the way that loss affected them terrify you?'

I immediately thought of my maternal grandma. My grandma lived to be ninety-two and had all her family around her till the end. She had an amazing marriage to my grandfather, who died about fifteen years before she did. But despite this seemingly wonderful old age, I still felt there was a constant sadness about her, because the passing of her beloved Harry was a void she couldn't fill, no matter how hard anyone tried or how full her life was. Such was their connection that she must have always felt he understood her and agreed with her views on life. Then, after he died, if anyone didn't hold the same point of view as her, it scared her, unnerved her and made her feel very alone. Whatever you said to her, even if it was something as superficial as, 'I like rah-rah skirts and ankle socks,' she would wrinkle her nose and say something like, 'Really? I just think it's so unfeminine, Katy!' But you could tell it was more than just fashion. She was actually thinking, 'I am no longer in synch with the people around me. Poor me. Nobody thinks like me any more.'

This made it hard to share what was really going on in your life, because you didn't want to upset her. The sadness at her loss was actually creating more isolation. And although we were close, I felt she was missing the chance to relate to her grandchildren and great-grandchildren on a new level. She didn't really want to engage with new friends either, as her older ones passed away. She kept saying, 'I just miss Harry.'

'But you know this,' said Annie, 'so you won't fall into that trap, or at least you can be aware of it. So why still be so scared? Is there something more?'

'Yes,' I said, suddenly seeing things more clearly. 'The effect it had on my mum.'

I think Grandma was quite a burden on my mother – physically and emotionally – although Mum would never concede this. Three or four times a week Mum would take several different buses to get from Abingdon to Swindon, where my grandmother lived, to take care of her. I don't think my dad relished her going – I think he understood and supported her doing it, but he had not long before taken early retirement and now Mum wasn't there as much as he would have liked. I always felt my mum was so torn, trying to do her best for the married life she had created with my dad, yet still doing the best for her mum. Grandma resisted any attempt to move her closer to their home, but also hated being left on her own. So Mum did this terrible journey that was always full of emotion, leaving my dad and her life at one end and at the other, my grandma pleading (even if not always saying out loud), 'Why do you have to leave?'

'And?' said Annie, really excited now. 'Come on, keep going – we're really getting somewhere!'

'And ... And ... I feel terrified, because one day I will be faced with the same. And I don't know if I will be able to be such a good daughter to my mum as she was to hers. I'm terrified she will have the same sadness, or my dad will, if he is a widower, and I won't know how to make it better. It raises so many questions. What if either wants to live with Derek and me when the other has gone – how would I feel about that? How would Derek? What if he said no? How could I refuse my parents? Would I have to choose between my parents and my married life? And what about my children? And ... And ...' I paused to catch my breath. 'I feel guilty,' I finally blurted out, 'guilty that I still have my parents when others don't, and guilty that I am even seeing their care as they get older as anything other than a joy and an honour when they have done so much for me.'

I couldn't breathe again. It was so freaky – I had to stop talking, because my throat closed up. Annie kept on tapping and said, 'Right, we're changing it now ...'

She encouraged me to say, 'Even though I have this guilt and fear about not being able to look after my parents in the way I feel I should and I'm very scared of the future, I totally love and accept myself.'

I felt completely exhausted after talking about all of this. A lot of these thoughts I had never actually allowed myself to think about before, let alone put into words. 'I'm going to give you some spiritual healing, because that was pretty intense,' Annie said. While I lay down for a rest, she massaged my feet and cleared my chakras by channelling her own energy. To my surprise, I felt a surge of joy and a new energy afterwards.

It was an amazing session. Annie helped me unlock what I find fearful, break it down and tease it apart. It was a great way to release instinctual fears and I was able to let some of the anxiety go and feel much calmer. I have a tendency to over-analyse things, so when I tried to write down my thoughts and fears in preparation for the session, it was all coming from the front of my brain. After I put myself in Annie's hands, a lot of stuff came out that I wouldn't otherwise have had access to. For me, it was a massive breakthrough in dealing with a wall of fear that couldn't be explained by all my logic and journalism. I imagine you could get a similar effect with a good therapist, or in other ways perhaps – using mindfulness, prayer or meditation – because the key is forcing yourself to stop and think about what's really bothering you, in an unconscious rather than intellectual way.

I decided then that I had to share my feelings with Derek. I had to know if he was going to support me in whatever was coming down the line, and back me if I wanted to open up our lives to having any of our parents living with us.

'My views on old age are different to yours,' he said, when I finally plucked up the courage. 'I would never expect Darcey or Billy to care for me and would be absolutely fine with them checking me into a home. Anything else would make me feel like a burden. Our society isn't really geared up for people to care for their parents full time. We all live miles apart and work longer and later in life, so aren't free to become full-time carers.'

'But that's no reason not to try!' I wailed. 'I hate that that's where our society is at. It seems wrong to put our children or our romantic relationships before our parents. It seems to me that our society is fundamentally mucked up and that we should place more emphasis on caring for our older people. So I want to welcome my parents if they want to come and live with me, because I think it's right. It should be possible to make it happen.'

'Of course it should,' Derek agreed. 'I would always support you in whatever you thought best. I love your parents and they will always be welcome, but I am not sure their moving in totally would be right for us or for them. Your mum or dad would then be locked in our world. Would they want that? I think you should talk to them about the whole subject.'

I was very scared of confronting this with my mum and dad, despite our closeness. Even mentioning them dying seemed wrong, like I was accepting it was going to happen when I would much rather put my head in the sand – and what if it upset *them*? But as is so often the case when we confront our worries head on, it was actually very liberating.

My mum said I had viewed her long emotional journeys to care for grandma very differently to how she had experienced them. She had actually enjoyed having time to herself on the bus, and relished the time with her mum, feeling she was doing all she could and making the most of every minute. Yes, there was sadness – sadness that she couldn't solve grandma's sense of loss and her own grief at the loss of her dad – but actually the trips helped her to deal with it. She could focus on my grandma while she was there, then on my dad and *their* life when she got back, and the long bus journeys allowed her to process the gap between the two worlds.

My dad, interestingly, said he had thought a lot about being alone while Mum was away on those trips, and it had made him think what it would be like if she had passed away. But he was pleased that she was doing it for grandma's sake. He said if he found himself alone, he would love to come and stay with my brother and me for regular visits and have us to stay with him, but he would want to carry on living his life at home for as long as he could, and if health problems affected this, he would meet them as it came to them. He also said he was glad we could talk like this because his mum had never been able to open up to him after his dad died – she just seemed to slip away into her own thoughts. This was something he was regretful and sad about – and something else I hadn't properly picked up on, because my worries over my mum's experiences were too dominant.

I felt good that I could reassure them that they would always be welcome. As usual, talking things through had really helped.

Back at the session with Annie, we had had a really interesting discussion about how I dealt with my fears. 'You've had throat problems for a long time,' Annie said, 'so it's weird that much of your professional life has been about speaking and using your voice. Does your mother talk a lot?'

'Yes,' I laughed, 'and my grandmother did too.'

'I think you come from a long line of people who have talked through their anxieties,' she went on. 'Even though you've had this history of problems, you've powered through it by talking, almost without trying, which is something we recommend. That has kept these fears at bay for most of your life, but in midlife they bubble up and force themselves to be heard. If you don't allow it, they will consume you. Usually, people who have very blocked throat chakras have been very controlled and maybe even denied a voice. You've always had a voice, but you've also spent your career using it to report on events, effectively telling other people's stories. I wonder if you've felt that you couldn't really speak up, share really important things about yourself or be yourself.'

She could be right. Maybe this book is my attempt to change that.

I left Annie feeling better than I had in a long time. In thinking about the end of my life – and my grand-parents' and parents' lives and deaths – I had clarified my worries. I had realised that a lot of my anxiety came from fear of loneliness and loss, and my morals and feelings about the way the world should be and the reality of the effects of that on all the other relation-ships in my life. By imagining the worst and planning for it, and working my way backwards, I felt a lot calmer and better.

I still had a lot to work out, but already the future seemed clearer.

CHAPTER 12

Finding Your Sparkle

By now, I felt I'd addressed quite a lot of frightening things on my journey through the realities of midlife. Something had shifted in me and I was feeling much happier about the future, which meant I was in a better place to discover all the positives it had to offer. All the research I'd done meant that my outlook had broadened. Now it was time to check my point of view and find my joy and purpose in midlife and beyond.

If there's one thing my job in breakfast telly gives you, it's a sense of perspective. Every time you start to grumble, you meet someone who has it worse. Every time you feel you have achieved something, there is a greater hero sitting next to you on the sofa with a story that leaves you speechless.

A few years ago, I visited Camp Zaatari on the Syrian–Jordanian border and sat in a tent with a woman who had nothing. Two weeks earlier, she had been in her home in Syria. Her husband was an architect and they had a comfortable home and a nice normal life with their four children. Then fighting came to her neighbourhood and her husband and eldest son were killed, so she took her remaining three children and fled on foot over the mountains and across the Jordanian border to seek refuge in the ever-growing United Nations refugee camp. All she had in the world was the tent that the UN Refugee Agency had given her, the dusty clothes on her back and the basic rations the camp had provided. Yet she offered to share her food with me.

I immediately said no, as I didn't want to take what little she had. But the UN translator explained that it would be better if I did. Sharing food and being a good host was central to Syrian culture and if I didn't accept her hospitality, I was taking away the only thing she had left of herself and her values. So I accepted and listened to her terrible stories of lost loved ones and destroyed lives, which she delivered with the proviso that she was hopeful things would now get better, and that she was grateful for the small mercies she had experienced. It was very humbling.

Back in the UK at the ITV breakfast studios, I was waiting to go on-air as part of a series of reports telling her story and that of the other extraordinary men, women and children I had met in the camp. I could hear a kerfuffle in the corridors where our dressing rooms are, so I poked my head round the corner. An almighty row was going on between a celebrity (who shall remain nameless) and a runner.

The celebrity was kicking off because we had run out of her favourite type of tea, some kind of herbal concoction. She was saying that it was 'the last straw!' Not only had she had to get up 'ludicrously' early, but there had already been no gluten-free toast, as she had 'specifically requested', and now this 'tea disaster'.

Given what I had seen in the refugee camp, the comparison was stark. I wanted to scream at the top of my voice, 'Disaster?! Are you kidding me? Do you have any idea how lucky you are, you revolting, ungrateful creature?'

But by now she had snatched the 'wrong tea' out of the runner's hand and slammed the door in his face, so I decided instead to console the runner, who was looking mortified and shaken. 'Don't worry, I saw everything. You didn't do anything wrong. It's totally her problem, not yours. She is clearly a very unhappy person.' Which, of course, she was.

The whole episode reminded me of that age-old philosophical question: who is to be more pitied, the paralysed man who has a naturally optimistic, happy nature, or the able-bodied man, consumed by gloom and pessimism? I have pondered this question quite a lot and I am still not sure of the answer. But I know which one I would rather hang out with.

My psychologist husband would say they are both prisoners, trapped in circumstances they cannot control, just like my woman in the refugee camp and the celebrity who was so consumed by her own inner demons. She couldn't enjoy what she had.

My friend of twenty years, Vanessa Ewbank, who now works as a producer in the entertainment department at *Good Morning Britain*, knows all about perspective. One minute she was nearly forty-five and worrying about all the superficial things that come with ageing, like crow's feet and grey hair – the next she was diagnosed with multiple sclerosis and prematurely facing some of the challenges of failing health that older people come up against.

'I used to feel jealous of people who were younger than me because of their gorgeous wrinkle-free skin,' she said. 'Now, as I take a taxi to work, with my wheel-chair in the back, I'm jealous of people of any age who are walking down the street, because they can just get up, walk off and grab a coffee. I miss all of the things I used to take for granted.'

How do people cope with such an unfair swipe from fate? I wondered this for the millionth time at the 2016 WellChild awards, which honours young children with serious illnesses, children who are carers, and the healthcare professionals who move mountains to support and look after them. Prince Harry is the patron and the annual WellChild awards ceremony recognises the courage of all these amazing people at a huge, sparkling event at a big London hotel.

I was sharing a table with one of the award winners, Jessica Davis, and her family. Jessie has a muscle-wasting disease, her mum has muscular dystrophy and her brother has psychotic episodes. They were all very excited to be there because it was a really spangly occasion, attended by stars like Sir Rod Stewart and his wife, Penny Lancaster, and Prince Harry himself.

Jessie's dad is the only family member without health problems. 'How on earth do you stay positive?' I asked him.

'What choice do we have?' he said.

'But how do you do it?' I pressed.

'Well, the one thing we know is that we have to stand by each other and look out for each other,' he explained. 'It forces us to enjoy every single moment when things aren't terrible – and take every opportunity to laugh.'

'How do you stop yourself going around moaning about your lot?'

'By realising that then we would have no friends, as well as a difficult life!' he joked.

It's hard to believe that some people can stay so positive when other people can't cope with the littlest things. Jessie and her family have had to face what is important to them, which is being with each other and taking the best of what they can along the way. They accept that things won't always be as good as they could be, but it's worth it to have each other. There's a combination of acceptance, making the most of the moment and prioritising what they want.

'You have to treat every small victory as a total triumph,' her father told me. 'You have to laugh, laugh, laugh.'

They say it's the best medicine – and it's scientifically proven that laughing is good for you on all kinds of levels. It relaxes you and releases endorphins (natural painkillers) into the bloodstream. It reduces the stress hormone, cortisol, and boosts your immune cells. It can also improve muscle tone and increase your oxygen levels, and – depending on how hard and long you laugh – it also gives you a bit of a cardiovascular workout. Amazingly, it doesn't have to spring from real glee. The body can't distinguish between fake and spontaneous laughter, so you get stress relief either way.

'I read that children laugh hundreds of times a day, whereas adults only manage about fifteen,' my friend Clare Lafferty told me.

And smiling? Smiling releases neuropeptides, which fight off stress, as well as three fabulous feel-good neurotransmitters: endorphins, dopamine and serotonin. A smile is not a one-way street, either, because when someone sees you smile – as long as you're not wielding an axe or a machete – it activates their orbitofrontal cortex, the part of the brain that is thought to process sensory rewards, among other emotions. And so they feel rewarded at the sight of your smile. It's why smiling is contagious.

I decided that I was going to try to smile as often as I could, in the hope that it would remind me to THINK HAPPY.

But it's hard to keep that in mind when daily life chips away at you – like when you're shattered and you come in from work thinking, I've got to get the washing done and send emails and I haven't got enough time!

'Can we go on Dad's computer?' the children asked me, one such evening.

'Yes,' I said, and felt a bit guilty. I knew they shouldn't really be on their screens, but it was also a relief because it meant I could clean up and put the washing on.

While I was downstairs panicking that I hadn't done the tea, I heard them laughing their socks off upstairs. I went up to see what was going on. 'What are you doing?'

'Watching a YouTuber,' they giggled.

Oh no, something else I don't really understand, I thought.

There's a whole batch of YouTubers that my kids are obsessed with, like Zoella, Thatcher Joe and Alfie Deyes. I hovered for a minute, you know, just to check what they were watching, and realised I had never really seen this side of YouTube before. Until then, all I'd picked up on was daft bloopers and crazy antics with cats in sunglasses, but suddenly I could see why my two loved these YouTubers. Unlike a lot of so-called 'real' kids' TV, which of course is largely written by adults and performed by actors, and is often full of teen trauma, scratchy rows and prank-playing, these guys were full of fun. Yes, they were cool and impossibly gorgeous, but they also exuded an innocent joy. They clearly loved the lives they'd made for themselves and, whether they were talking about buying scented candles from the supermarket, stringing up fairy lights to make 'everything pretty' or playing essentially old-school parlour games with a new trendy twist, their warmth and enthusiasm bounced out of the screen. I found myself laughing, too.

'Let's play these games ourselves!' the children said, having been inspired by the YouTubers' antics. 'You too, Mum!'

I started to say, 'I haven't got time. There's the tea and the washing to do, and then homework ...'

'Please, Mum! Can't we have sandwiches and fruit and play games instead?'

I paused for a second, torn between duty and fun. Bugger it, I thought, I'll stay.

It was one of those turning-point moments. For the first time I felt that, rather than being the teacher introducing my children to the world, I was letting my kids teach me something new, take *me* into a new world and teach me about being a mum, too. We played a game called 'Chubby Bunnies', where you take turns putting marshmallows into your mouth for a laugh, and we ended up being stupid for hours. It wasn't how I had planned for the evening to go, but it didn't matter.

The children absolutely loved it, and I realised that they rarely saw me being silly. They saw me trying to be entertaining and creating fun for them, but actually just being silly when they wanted to be – not when was convenient – was really important. And then Derek came in from work and we forced him to play too.

'I don't like this. I'm going to be sick!' he complained, and we fell about laughing.

It was totally daft, the sort of silliness I associated with the drinking games I played as a student. Normally, you just don't do that stuff in midlife. Nothing like it. You're too bowed down by responsibility. But I love the idea of doing stupid things with your partner, or your kids, so that you giggle your butts off together. It's a really good idea to make time for fun. I'm not talking about a massage because you need it because you're stressed (it's just another thing to put in your diary) but really stupid stuff. Something ridiculous that serves you no advantage whatsoever.

Yes, you've got to build in time to relax – take time out, light a candle, have a bath – but it's also got to be more daft than that. Breaking a responsible midlife mindset is a critical part of getting our heads right. Of course, you don't want to drink until four in the morning, because it's knackering and you'll be hung-over for days, but you've got to get daftness back. It's something I don't do because, like so many people, I'm scheduled to the max – but I think you have to create time and space for yourself in midlife. It's important to have moments when you slow down.

I remember asking the actress Julia Roberts about making time for herself and her children. Before I met her, I'd been thinking how difficult it must be to spend time away filming for long periods, especially when the temptation must be there to buy her children a million things to make up for it.

'We have a tiny plot of ground in our garden and we go out there and plant things,' she told me. Of course, she added, her children always want to see the kind of instant results they get on their apps on their phones, but with gardening it sometimes takes weeks, or years. 'I just find it forces all of us to slow right down, including me,' she said.

This was something I loved doing with my parents as I was growing up – and now that we've moved house and finally have a garden rather than a concrete back yard, I've been talking to the children about what we want to grow in it. So far we've laid out a tiny vegetable patch and planted a border. We've had a lot of fun collecting fruit from the little apple and pear trees, too.

There's something about digging and planting that brings you back to yourself, perhaps because it is a slow, laborious process. This is crucial, because the gap between our real selves and the made-to-order selves we've constructed to get by in the world is perhaps at its widest in midlife. Intrinsic to my idea of mastery is that you have to find your own way, rather than performing for others. It is you who is driving the bus. Not your parents, teachers, peers and bosses. The old rules no longer apply in this new era.

So I began trying get in touch with being completely authentic, with somewhat disastrous consequences. Not that I have ever been fake, of course – far from it – but there are times, you know, when you feel it's better not to fully speak up, perhaps to tell the odd white lie. My mum calls it 'Kate glossing'. Not any more.

So when my husband emerged ready to make a big speech for his work and said, 'I haven't worn this black velvet jacket for ages – is it too tight? Can I get away with it?' I replied, 'Not really, darling, you have put on loads of weight recently. That button is straining and it makes you look even fatter.'

'Thanks,' he said. 'I was already feeling nervous. Now I can't wear my good luck jacket, either.'

'Just being honest,' I chirped.

When Laura Tobin, *Good Morning Britain*'s adorable and super-clever weather presenter, made a batch of cakes as part of a *Great British Bake Off* item, everyone in the *GMB* morning editorial meeting tried them and said how dry they were. So when Laura asked later, 'What did everyone think of my cakes?' rather than saying, 'Oh, we all thought it was very kind of you to make them,' or something typically 'Kate glossing' that would avoid a brutal answer, I said, 'Everyone thought they were dry, I'm afraid.'

She looked crushed. 'But that's only because they'd been out for hours,' she protested

I felt dreadful. 'Just being honest,' I said, but quieter this time, under my breath.

I started to think that maybe this new full-force, no-holds-barred approach would work better if I kept it on-air, on *Good Morning Britain*, in journalist mode. I certainly had a good role model for it in my colleague Piers Morgan. I have known Piers for more than twenty years and am very fond of him. He has always shown me personally the incredibly kind, loyal side to his personality.

He also, I think, has a brilliant sense of humour. I knew him ten years before I met my husband, and he knew Derek separately from Derek's time in politics. When our engagement was announced, we walked into a big red carpet event and Piers took one look at me and said, 'Are you serious? You and Derek Draper? I mean, Derek bloody Draper, of all people. If I'd known your bar was set so low, I'd have had a crack myself!' Other people's fiancés may not have laughed, but fortunately Derek thought it was hysterical. We even used that quote on our wedding invite!

Not everyone, of course, relishes his manner and there's no doubt he knows how to ruffle feathers. Indeed, Piers arrived at *Good Morning Britain* like a tornado. In fact, we even called him the 'mini tornado' – and he objected to the 'mini'! He opens shows with attacks on senior, well-respected politicians; he speaks his mind to the nth degree, which is the antithesis of what I'd been trained to do as a news journalist. Of course, you can share your emotions or experiences, but you're not supposed to air your beliefs or say things from your personal point of view. So although I might say that I think something could be frightening for children, because that's an emotional response, I wouldn't say that it's wrong to do anything in a certain way, as I don't feel it's my place to tell people what to do. I am there to ask the questions. It is up to whoever is watching to form their opinions, I had always been taught.

Mind you, people still give you flak just for doing that. If you are dealing with sensitive issues, like those surrounding Brexit, and you are just asking questions and putting the opposing point of view to whoever you are interviewing, people can get really irate and confuse the line of questioning with your own personal opinion. I find that so frustrating and want to say, 'It's a debate. I am just laying out the issues, not getting on a soap box!' But, of course, I can't.

Piers, though, appears to have no such restraint. He always gives his opinion on any subject, whether he is asked for it or not. Maybe it's his years as a columnist and experience as a tabloid editor, but he doesn't seem to care about the flak – he positively welcomes it. I have known him a long time, but working with him and watching him up close has made me realise that he has injected a life and an energy to the show in a very different way to the other presenters I have worked with. There is a liberation in what he does. He is carefree. He just goes ahead and says whatever, whenever, ignoring the producers, the viewers' reactions – everybody. And it is exhilarating. It made me wonder whether I should take a leaf out of his book.

A few days after this thought occurred to me, Ben Shephard and I interviewed Nicola Sturgeon, Scotland's first minister, during the Scottish National Party conference. Her first answer was about two minutes long and she didn't really address the question, but neither Ben nor I interrupted, even though the whole interview was meant to be about four minutes in total. It's very difficult to butt in when you're interviewing someone from a location outside the studio because there's often a satellite delay on the sound, so if you do interrupt, the person at the other end hears what you say a few seconds after you say it. So they keep on talking over you, then stop, by which time you have started to speak again, so they stop again and the whole thing becomes a jumbled mess! Another problem is that you haven't got the visual signal of looking at someone face to face, and so they can't see your expression and know you're about to ask a question or respond to what they're saying.

When she had finished, Ben explained, 'We don't want to interrupt you, but we are going to have to ask you that again, because you didn't really answer the question and we do have a limited time ...'

Now, Nicola Sturgeon was absolutely in full charge mode that day. She had been at a conference all week, delivering speeches, and she was taking a stand, which had pleased her party, by saying that she would call a second referendum if she didn't get what she wanted from the UK government. But the nature of our programme is that guests aren't there to make speeches. We have conversations – we ask questions and people answer them – and that's what Ben was hoping to encourage.

She began again, but it went the same way. My producers were saying in my ear, 'Just give up on this! It's really not working, you are not getting through and it's going on way too long.'

I decided that unless the people watching were Nicola Sturgeon fans and fully signed up card-carrying members of the SNP, hanging on her every word, they were probably thinking, blimey, she goes on a bit! And since my job is to say what people are thinking – and in the spirit of my new speak-up mode – I thought, let's try a joke to see if that breaks up the mood and makes it more of a conversation.

So I said, 'Everyone says I talk loads, Nicola, but you're seriously giving me a run for my money today. I'd love to ask you something else though, in the last minute we have ...'

But she didn't look amused. Afterwards, I was slaughtered for it on social media. People were saying, 'How dare you?'

'You shouldn't pay any attention if you get fewer than ten comments on Twitter,' Derek pointed out. 'That's just politically active people who are engaged to attack anyone who doesn't seem to be giving a total platform to the person they support.'

Having worked as a researcher in political broadcasting myself, I believe it, but as I don't generally get negative tweets, I was flummoxed, particularly as I had been taking a bit of a risk. And also because I really admire Nicola Sturgeon and would never want to be rude to her.

Afterwards, I wished I'd said, 'Everyone says I talk loads, Nicola, but you're seriously giving me a run for my money today. The difference is that I blather on about nothing whereas you've got interesting things to say.' I wished I'd turned it around and made the joke on myself. It may not have stopped the criticism, but it would have given her the chance to laugh along too and made me feel less uncomfortable.

The following week, Cheryl (formerly Cheryl Cole) was in the news. At the end of a very straight programme dealing with a lot of serious news, we came to Richard Arnold's entertainment section, which tends to be more lighthearted, and a welcome chance to laugh after such weighty issues. Richard was talking about the fact that Cheryl had said she'd put on weight because she was happier now, after losing weight in the period leading up to her separation from her second husband, Jean-Bernard Fernandez-Versini. A picture was put up on the screen of her looking very skinny and then a picture of her still looking incredibly slim.

In my head, I was thinking, gosh, the poor woman is under so much scrutiny and this is just making it worse! I experienced a little of it myself when I came back to work after Darcey was born and suddenly

I started to lose a dramatic amount of weight. It was later diagnosed as a severe overactive thyroid, but was very frightening, because at the time I was eating like a horse but still dropping pounds every day and didn't know why. I was scared something really serious was wrong. What made it worse was that viewers thought I was on some crazy post-pregnancy diet.

'Stupid cow,' they phoned in to say. 'Why is she trying to be size zero? Doesn't she realise she is risking her health and looks awful?' Or 'How pathetic that she is worried about shedding her mum tum when really all she should care about is her health and that of her baby!'

So I know all about the assumptions people can make about weight loss and how hurtful it can be. And I feared that, without meaning to, we were doing it on the show. So, because the entertainment section of the show is all about fun and giggles, I again tried to make a joke to highlight the point in a lighthearted way.

'Oh, yes, she's really ballooned!' I said, joking of course, as that was the exact opposite of they way she looked. 'Is that what counts as putting on weight in Cheryl's world? Good grief!' I said.

What I was intending to convey, in a light-hearted way was, 'Good grief, poor Cheryl. There's so much analysis over her weight. Thank goodness she looks happy, but really it's not as if she's ballooned now. She's still very slim.'

Nobody got the jokey attempt at irony, though, and before the hour was out four online newspapers were running stories saying that I had launched a scathing attack on Cheryl's weight gain. Then people who hadn't even seen the original comment on TV started commenting on the online reports, saying, 'How dare she attack Cheryl?' It was all very frustrating. It left me feeling rattled and shook my confidence about being less cautious and more outspoken.

Maybe I can't say out loud what's going through my mind, I thought.

I guess you have to decide whether you're the kind of person who can take the flak, and make sure that when you do speak up it's not just a flippant comment or a joke to ease the tension in a people-pleasing way, but actually something very clear. That, or brace yourself for criticism and be more like Piers Morgan, who lives and thrives on 50 per cent loathing and 50 per cent loving.

'Maybe I should make some sort of public apology,' I said aloud to myself, as I mulled it over after the show.

'Don't be ridiculous!' said Ben Shephard, who I hadn't realised was listening. 'You have done nothing wrong – anybody watching would have got where you were coming from if they had taken a moment to think about it. But I have noticed you are slightly different on the show recently – is something going on?'

So I explained.

'That's ridiculous!' he exclaimed again. 'Piers is Piers and you are you. You both bring something totally different to the show – a whole different set of skills. I think you should just be 100 per cent Kate Garraway. That's the person we all adore, and the real reason why you have had your job for twenty years.

'I think,' he continued, 'that while you have been so focused on your midlife maelstrom, addressing the stuff that you want to improve and change, you've been forgetting about all your amazing successes. All the stuff that your brand of skills has achieved. Shouldn't you be celebrating your triumphs, too? You have interviewed every prime minister since Margaret Thatcher, pretty much the whole of Hollywood's A-list – and didn't you get to do that because of your own approach to interviewing and your own presenting style? And weren't you the first person in the world to broadcast live from the pyramids in Egypt? Others had tried, but wasn't it you, with your quiet, dogged determination, who actually did it?'

'Yes,' I said, feeling weirdly shy about hearing some of my achievements trumpeted.

'So you don't have to be anything but you. Although to be the best, 100 per cent version of yourself, I can't help thinking you've got to get more sleep.'

He had a point. Part of the reason why my attempts at speaking my mind didn't work in the way I wanted is that I was shattered. The night before I blundered with Nicola Sturgeon I'd had about two hours' sleep, because Billy wasn't very well, and so I didn't deliver my thoughts fully or clarify my comments.

When I was younger I could function on two hours' sleep. Now I couldn't. I was aware that my brain didn't work as fast. So I needed to compensate.

I had overhauled my diet, become fitter through exercise and laid to rest a lot of demons from the past. But there was still the sleep dragon to slay.

It was going to mean some big changes. I'd have to start ruthlessly prioritising my time, reorganising the way I worked. It was likely to involve some awkward conversations with work colleagues and friends who I might have to disappoint by saying no to more often when they were used to me saying yes.

I was going to have to make a lot of changes at home too, including asking Derek to look after the kids more often, and do more around the house. It was going to be a big battle with myself and everyone else, as I have never been very good at saying no or asking for help. It felt a bit like being a teenager again, standing up to Mum and Dad for the first time, by saying, 'No, I'm not wearing that nice dress to Granny's for tea!' But I had already discovered that midlife is a bit like a second puberty – and in a way, the stakes this time around are even higher. I needed to find a voice and speak up for myself, even though I find confrontation scary.

I've always felt that relationships are based upon deals that you can't really break. Whether it's boss-to-employee, mother-and-child or friend-to-friend, you have relationships based on what you give them and they give you. I don't mean that in a cynical way, or a tit-for-tat way. It's just that you know where you are with people.

When Derek and I met, I was someone who was happy to get up early and run around even when I wasn't working, whereas Derek likes a lie-in. But I couldn't allow him to indulge that any more – he had to take up some of the slack if I was going to try to get more sleep and occasionally get a lie-in myself beyond 6 a.m. when the kids woke up. So the deal we originally made was changing. Sometimes, though, that happens as time moves on and things develop. The key is to be clear about what you want and why – and have the confidence to ask for it. How was he going to react?

'I need more sleep,' I said to him. 'You're going to have to get up earlier at weekends.'

His initial reaction was, 'I don't like the sound of that.'

It was a blow. I wanted him to give me a positive and supportive: 'Of course I'll help you!' Usually, because I hate confrontation, I would have let it drop at this point. But because I really needed it, I stood my ground, and insisted.

Luckily what is great about Derek is that although he may appear grumpy and not massively receptive at first, he will be more supportive once he's had time to think about it. He has a very busy and challenging working life too, so I hated having to keep bringing it up when he was tired at the end of a long day. But I carried on raising it again, over the days that followed, and we talked it through. Then it clicked, and he said, 'OK, of course I totally understand you need more sleep, I'll give it a go.'

It meant a change for him – but I think change is an inevitable challenge in midlife. It could be that you're in an unhappy relationship and you're trying to find your feet to adjust it, but even if you're in a happy relationship, there are changes to be faced. Your body is changing. You need to do more to stay the same – more sleep, maybe; you can't do as much. Your looks are changing and you may be worried you're not as attractive to your partner, or be finding them less attractive. Your needs within the relationship are changing too and this can affect its balance, all of which can be tricky to manage. So it's about working it out and not minding that people are not going to be instantly delighted necessarily – but pushing forward, firmly but gently, to get through it.

Sometimes you need to stay patient when you speak up, and realise that you may still need to compromise. One partner may say, 'I want to be a sculptor. I'm frustrated. I want a new life.' They rush off and go to a different class every night of the week. Meanwhile, their partner is thinking, 'Hang on a minute! I don't know where *I* am now – and what about having the chance to express *myself*?'

So, as I said at the beginning of this book, the key to mastering midlife and beyond is realising that you are driving the bus. And, yes, that is true. But you may well also have passengers – and you need to be kind to the other people on your journey.

There are tough conversations to be had in midlife, and not just with our partners and parents. It could be that your kids have got used to you subsidising their lives even though they are grown. If you're really stretched for cash and running yourself ragged working too hard to pay for them, you may have to face the fact you can't help them so much any more. You may have to say, 'Listen, we can't do it. We can't help with your rent.'

It's a horrible feeling of failure, in a way, but it's a conversation that creates much-needed space for you, and may help them to stand on their own two feet, too.

Finding your voice and speaking up will hopefully give you the confidence to try something new, which is vital to staying fresh in midlife. Keeping fresh was easy when you were young. You used to go round to your mate's house with a new album or magazine and say, 'Have you heard this? Seen this?' You were constantly introducing new music and ideas into your life, refreshing and renewing your influences.

But nobody does that in their forties or fifties. You don't go round to your mate's house and say, 'Listen to this. I love it.'

So you have to do it for yourself, otherwise you will become stale. It's not about being clued-in or cool now, though; it's about finding new thought processes and ideas that touch and reach you and keep you current. It's focusing on the positives of being young – the newness and excitement – and getting that back into your life instead of wishing you were actually young again. If you want to be fresh, you have to be open. It can be scary to take on a new challenge, to the extent that it might flood your body with adrenaline just to contemplate it, but it's worth it.

I have a test for deciding what is good and what is bad adrenaline. If I could get out of something and I choose to – like root canal surgery – that's bad adrenaline; if I could get out of it but I still want to do it, that's good adrenaline. When I first got my job at Smooth Radio I had to learn to mix music as a DJ, something I had never done as a journalist. I had to face my technology fears and be trained to use all the new equipment, and 'drive' the music mixing desk on my own, which was completely alien to me – and no mean feat for someone who can barely park a car! What made it worse was that I couldn't even debrief about it to my friends in the business afterwards over a glass of wine – I had to be trained in total secret so that there could be a big announcement before my first show. They didn't want anybody in the building to know that I was going to be the new person on the new brand, so I had to go in at three in the morning and be trained by Dave Brierley-Jones who is now my producer. We hid out in one of the less-used old studios, where he showed me a few basic things, like using the faders and how to mix a song from one to another.

'Right, I'll leave you to play around while I go and grab some more music,' he said, and off he went.

While he was away, I swept my hand across the desk and accidentally spilt an entire caffè latte over the decks. Grabbing my script, I started dabbing furiously, but the script turned out to be surprisingly non-absorbent and there was no kitchen roll to be found. It was a disaster.

Dave came back. 'Are you all right?' he asked. He cocked his head slightly. 'Hang on a minute, what's that buzz?'

'I'm really sorry, but I might have spilt a little bit of coffee on the desk,' I said.

'How much?' he snapped.

I was really scared. 'I'm not sure. Maybe just a little bit.'

'OK, there's definitely a buzz. Did it go anywhere near the faders?'

I gulped. 'To be honest, I think it did go a little bit near one fader,' I said, knowing that the entire grande latte had gone INTO *all* the faders.

He grimaced. 'Don't worry, it's a really old studio and they're going to refit it soon,' he said, kindly trying to make me feel better. 'But I'm going to have to report it ...'

He reported that he'd been doing some work in the studio and some liquid had been spilt in the desk. When the engineers came in the next morning, they found that the whole thing was fried. They were really cross that someone had ruined their beautiful equipment, so they pulled the security camera video, which had just about captured me in the background, but from the back view, so they didn't recognise me. They took it to Dave and said, 'Who was this?'

'Oh my God!' he said as he watched it back. 'She said it was just a little bit!'

It was an old studio and hopefully it was insured, but people still like to rub it in. Every time I see the boss, Mike Osborne, he says, 'You cost me the price of a small family car before you even went on-air!'

After such an inauspicious start, it would have been easy for me to give up (and for them to give up on me!) and to go home, confidence shattered. But I thought, no, I've got to stick at it.

Even now, I would say that I'm not the best on-air. There are far better DJs technically, but I've learnt to do it. I can make it work and it's given me a whole new string to my bow, a new lease of life, a new revenue stream plus I get to hear my favourite music every day. And maybe luckiest of all, you can't see wrinkles on the radio!

A far more terrifying adrenaline test was the first time I rode a motorbike. Now, I am not a natural biker. The combination of no balance and my utter lack of physical courage makes me singularly unsuitable. Thank goodness I wasn't actually driving the thing – I was clinging to a very experienced biker who runs a kind of motorbike taxi service.

Ceri picked me up at Heathrow Airport. I had flown out to New York to interview the singer Amy Winehouse's dad, shortly after she had died. I interviewed him and then fed the footage back to London from ITV's edit suite in Manhattan. The plan was then to jump on a plane, grab a few hours' sleep in flight and head back to present the segment on what was then called *Daybreak*, back in the UK. But just as I was getting on the flight at JFK, the producer rang.

'We have a problem,' he said. 'With the time difference, you don't land until after 6 a.m. and with the traffic at that time in the morning, there is no way you are going to get from Heathrow to the centre of London before we go off air at 8.30.'

I resisted the urge to ask why no one had thought of this before.

'But we do have a solution,' he continued. 'You could get a limo bike.'

Maybe it was the fact I had been up and working now for thirty-six hours straight – or maybe it was the thought that Mitch Winehouse's story wouldn't be properly heard if I didn't do this (he'd poured his aching heart and soul out to me) – but I nervously agreed.

Standing in the rain outside Heathrow, though, I wasn't so sure. Burly Ceri with his massive motorbike smiled reassuringly. 'Everyone is nervous the first time. David Cameron was, but now he loves it.'

I thought, well, if it's good enough for a prime minister …

'And anyway, there is an intercom in the helmet so you can talk to me and tell me if you want me to slow down.'

'Slow down!' I shrieked, as we left the car park.

'Kate, we are going eleven miles an hour. I have to go a *bit* faster otherwise we are never going to get there.'

'OK, but I'm warning you, I am going to scream.'

And scream I did – loudly and blood-curdlingly. After ten minutes Ceri turned the intercom off. Presumably his ears were bleeding.

God knows what people thought to hear me screaming all the way, but as we made the forty-five-minute journey into London, the rain stopped, the sun came up and I began to see the benefit of motorbike riding. It was exciting weaving through the traffic and the adrenaline made everything seem brighter and shinier somehow. Soon afterwards, I started using limo bikes regularly to get from ITV to Smooth so that I could get there to be on-air on my radio show by 10 a.m., and I realised that this way of travelling offers a unique perspective on life. I can't look at my phone, read or go to sleep because I'm too busy hanging on. I'm exposed enough and going slowly enough to feel part of the city and connected. And I've met some amazing people along the way. There's something about sitting with your thighs wrapped around a virtual stranger that makes for some very intimate chats! I know so much about Pete's daughter's training to be a social worker that I felt as proud as if she was my own when she got a distinction. I've revelled in Damien's wild tales of his former life as a motorbike racer. And Rhys even introduced me to a new set of underwear – just when I thought I had worn every big knicker going! He told me his little secret to keeping warm in winter on the bike was to wear battery-powered electrically heated under-garments. I went out and bought them immediately and they almost literally saved my life when I covered Donald Trump's presidential inauguration in January 2017. Standing outside for hours on end on a roof top in Washington, with a serious wind chill making it feel colder than the North Pole, meant some correspondents were worried about hypothermia setting in. But not me in my toasty tighty-whities – thanks, Rhys! All this, again, proving that opening up rather than narrowing down your experiences is the path to a richer, more fascinating life.

It's important to learn your limits, know how far to push yourself and not be afraid to say something is too much for you. Midlife is the perfect time to test all of this, because when you were younger you might have gone too far and maybe when you're older you might not push yourself far enough. As for me, I say no to motorways, but I'm prepared to get on the bike.

My friend, Nick Harris, took the plunge in a different way. He has always worked behind the cameras as a director, but a few years ago he suddenly thought, 'I'm forty-one. What am I going to do with the rest of my life?'

He didn't have a long-term partner or any children, so he didn't have to worry about the immediate direct impact on anyone else from a big life change, but it did mean personal sacrifices. 'I've always wanted to act,' he thought, 'and I don't want to feel later on that I haven't done something I wanted to do – so I'm going to give it a try.'

He tried out for drama school and got in, squeezing it in around other commitments, which meant very long days and putting on hold other areas of his life. But now, at forty-four, he is with the RSC doing small parts in a couple of Shakespeare plays. And he is having the best time ever! He says about four lines over the course of a night, but he doesn't care. 'Maybe the work will dry up in a few years' time – and I still have to work in other jobs to pay the bills – but the point will be that I've done it,' he told me. 'It's incredibly liberating to realise you don't HAVE to stick to the career path you've been on for a long time. Shake up your life – reinvigorate it – and at the same time be mindful of keeping old doors ajar so you can go back if you need to.'

The flip side of branching out like Nick is accepting what you can't do and coming to terms with it. There's absolutely no point in moaning that you're in a job where the money is bad and the boss is horrible. Instead, think, well, WHY am I staying? Is it really because I have no choice? Or is it because the hours kind of suit me and if I am honest with myself I actually don't want any more responsibility while I'm busy with my family or whatever at this time in my life?

Think about your options and maybe retrain, but don't make an enemy of your life as it is. If the job actually suits your needs for the time being, accept your decision to stick with it.

Think, OK, this job isn't as rewarding as I would like and doesn't pay as much money as I would like, but on another level I can fit it in around picking the kids up from school, or seeing my friends, or doing a hobby I love. Therefore, I'm not going to moan about it; it's my decision.

If you've always been too scared to try something different, then maybe now is the time to do something new, rather than waiting around for fate to land something on your lap. But if you realise you're making a conscious, expedient compromise, it makes it easier to put up with whatever you have for now and make a note to yourself to think about something else in the future. Don't beat yourself up about not being exactly where you want to be right now. You do have the time to change it when you are ready. Make peace with yourself.

One of the things I'm making peace with is the fact that I can't do everything. I have to get more sleep now. I remember a week when I would have liked to take up my invites to go on *8 Out of 10 Cats* and to the Pride of Britain's sports awards, two things I would have loved to do and felt I should do. But I knew if I did, I wouldn't have been rested enough to do the things I was already committed to – work and being a mum. So I just couldn't. Still, I didn't see it as losing out, and still don't. I refuse to dwell on whether I'm missing out on fun or a potential career opportunity. In fact, I see it as a gain: gaining sleep – and, with it, freshness and vitality, to make the most of the good luck and the good things I already have in my life.

Choosing to see your life from a different perspective can lead to a whole new path, or in my case, lead to a renewed purpose in travelling the road I am already on. It's all down to perspective, and the joy is that we are in sole control of it.

CHAPTER 13

And Finally ... The Real Joy of B.I.G. K.N.I.C.K.E.R.S!

So what have I learnt from this adventure and my attempts to master my midlife? Well, over the past year I realised I have come to embrace a subtle yet present and personal power. It brings a faint, warming glow to my heart, and also a familiar flutter like when you wake up on Christmas morning as a kid, or go on a youthful first date; the excitement of something new – a flutter I had not felt in a long while. The future is not set, for me or anyone else.

Every experience from my past, from a few days ago to many decades before, has been an investment in the moment I live in right now. Just as your past has for you too! So we could feel that fifty and beyond is the autumn of life and find it depressing, because autumn is about leaves falling off trees, things dying and winter coming. Or, instead of a time of decay, we can see it as harvest time, when we are reaping the fruits of the first half of our lives.

So as I step forward into midlife and beyond, I have decided to pick from all I have learnt but, as importantly, discard all regrets that I now have no power to change. And this is the art of mastery for me: the reaped fruit that I choose to bring to my present contribute positively (and only positively) to the choices I make in the here and now, and the future. I have sole responsibility and sole power to do this.

From stuffing marshmallows in my mouth and laughing with my wonderful children to having those tricky conversations with my husband and parents, I can consciously make choices each moment of my day to create a fresh, joyous and exciting path.

A path not yet set!

So now whenever I feel my perspective is getting skewed or I am getting lost again in the maelstrom of midlife, I have a checklist I run through to remind myself to stay on track. It fits very handily into the acronym of B.I.G. K.N.I.C.K.E.R.S. Well, it would, wouldn't it? And I would love to share it with you.

B is for 'Be prepared'. I need to take stock and plan for the worst, so worries don't obscure the best outcome. Be prepared to face my fears – work out what is really troubling me and face up to it, so I can free myself from those fearful shadows.

I stands for 'I' – not being too afraid to put myself first. When an air hostess runs through the emergency procedures on a plane, they always say that adults must put their oxygen masks on first before fitting them to their children. That's because you are not in a position to help others if you cannot breathe yourself. So don't feel selfish: take care of yourself.

G is for 'Give away the past'. Not forget it. It's part of me and a step on my journey, but it is not going to define my future. I mentally give away what I know isn't helping me any more.

K is for 'Kindness'. Be kind to myself and to others. I believe there is an extraordinary, almost magical, power in kindness, and when we are frazzled and fraught through lack of time, it's easy to forget to be kind. Kindness is obviously great for those on the receiving end of it, but also for the giver. Taking time to be kind forces me to slow down and be mindful. It helps me feel connected to the people around me, less isolated in a mad, modern world and brings those wonderful moments of joy when I know I am part of something good.

N is for 'New masters' – that's us! Parents, bosses, teachers and bullies don't define us any more, nor does society say what we must be. I define myself. I face up to my fears, take responsibility for my own actions and become my own master.

I is for 'Innovate'. Stay fresh, keep an open mind and constantly introduce myself to new things – even if, having experienced them, I then decide they are not for me.

C is for 'Choice' – never forget I always have choice. Choice in how I perceive the challenges of life, choice in how I view where life has led me and who with. Choice to let it neither confine nor define me. And choice to make peace with the choices of the past. Oh, and C is also for 'Celebrate'! I should celebrate my triumphs, however big or small, as they remind me to take joy in what I have achieved and to be grateful for the positives I have in my life.

K is for 'Krazy'! Crazy with a capital 'k'! By which I mean silliness and fun, too often lost in midlife. I need to keep it with me and, if lost, go and find it again or try it for the first time!

E is for 'Energy'. In midlife we worry so much about time – that time is running out or that we haven't got enough time in the day. But I have learnt that if I focus less on my *decreasing* amount of time and more on *increasing* my energy, then I have more time, because I have the energy to do the things I need to do and the energy to enjoy what time I have. Find a diet and exercise routine that works to give you the energy you need – you deserve it!

R is for 'Relationships' ... and 'Romance' too. I have to remember that all relationships, romantic or otherwise, are not set. They are always changing – they have to, whether we want them to or not. By their very nature, relationships are made between people, and people's needs and wants will inevitably change with time. I have to remember to Reconnect, Reinvent, Rekindle and Renew.

S is for 'Stillness', 'Silence', 'Space' and 'Sleep'. However fraught our midlives, I try to remember the power of silence and stillness, and indulge in it every day. I always have earplugs in my bag now wherever I go, so that even if I only have ten minutes before a meeting or waiting for the kids to come out of school, I pop them in and force myself to think of a Soothing image, like waves crashing on the beach. Doing this has given me more Space to Sparkle.

This is my absolute joy in 'Big Knickers'. Just like my real big knickers that I wear to please myself, not anyone else. They are my little secret, tucked underneath as I go about my daily life, stretchy and comfy, keeping me toasty warm and helping me to feel sexy by smoothing my lumps and bumps. So too my B.I.G. K.N.I.C.K.E.R.S. checklist is my new secret discovery, uncovered through my adventures as I approached my fiftieth birthday. I may not shout about it from the rooftops (or flash it on TV!); I keep it tucked away with me to help me feel at my best and make the best of what's to come, to love the rest of my life. That's the real joy in Big Knickers – it's the joy of a Big Life, whatever your age!

Thank you for letting me share with you my story of trying to master my midlife and beyond. I hope it will help you to feel you are making the most of your own. I would love you to share your story with me, too, and you can get in touch with me at www.facebook.com/kategarraway. For now, though – goodbye and good luck!